"Exponential growth in information is limited without platforms and networks to amplify and leverage its impact. As two of our nation's outstanding education leaders, Tom and Lydia explain the power and intentionality of connecting people and organizations to help them learn and grow."

— *Vince M. Bertram, Ed.D., MBA,*
President and CEO, Project Lead The Way

"A wise superintendent once said, 'Isolation is the enemy of improvement.' This invaluable book provides a powerful rationale, great examples, and incredibly useful guidelines for genuine innovation networks among teachers and schools. It should be in every education leader's toolbox.

—*Tony Wagner, author of* The Global Achievement Gap *and* Creating Innovators

"I am a strong believer that we need networks and professional learning communities to learn and share from each other in managing the changes needed for education transformation. Creating a dialog for advancing contemporary approaches to rethink school models, how teachers teach and the demands on learning for our students is critical. This drive to transform demands collective capacity-building and deeper learning by adults around shifting practices and mindsets to create change. This book offers valuable insights on why networks for leading change matters and the ways educators will leverage networks to expand access to powerful, innovative learning models, preparing each student for success in college, career, and life."

—*Susan Patrick, President and CEO of iNACOL,*
co-founder of CompetencyWorks

"Brilliant work! We all know that we are better when we work together. However, the most forward thinking educators often choose to trailblaze alone. *Better Together* is a must read for anyone engaged in school reform."

—*Dr. Timothy S. Stuart, Head of School at the International Community School of Addis Ababa, and co-author of* Personalized Learning in a PLC at Work: Student Agency Through the Four Critical Questions *(Solution Tree, 2018)*

"Education can no longer rely on hub and spoke methods of distributing learning. Learning is happening at a faster pace in a networked world. Across the 500 schools we work with the most successful schools are collaborating across schools within their district and across the country. Tom and Lydia provide examples a taxonomy of networks which increases learning and helps schools attain their goals."

—*Anthony Kim, CEO of Education Elements & co-author of* The New School Rules

"A tour de force through the most cutting-edge ideas, schools, and educators, *Better Together* not only gives the 101 on the concepts educators and citizens need to understand, but also how they can be enacted effectively in schools."

—*Michael Horn, Chief Strategy Officer, The Entangled Group, Distinguished Fellow of the Clayton Christensen Institute, and author of* Disrupting Class *and* Blended

"For a long time education reformers have focused on improving individual institutions—getting the best people at the helm of a school, solidifying the culture, and implementing best practices—in a siloed manner. Vander Ark and Dobyns show how limiting that approach can be. *Better Together* illustrates the power of learning on common platforms that connect networks of like-minded schools and institutions. At long last the whole of schools' efforts to innovate and improve could be great than the sum of its parts."

—*Julia Freeland Fisher, Director, Education, at Clayton Christensen Institute*

"Tom Vander Ark and Lydia Dobyns have been working in the education trenches to find practical and realistic approaches to improve outcomes for kids as long and as thoughtfully as anyone. I highly recommend this excellent book, as school networks enable us to move past 'one-off innovations' and create paths for schools to sustain great work and share their learning together. This book and Vander Ark's and Dobyns' expert views should move to the top of the list for educators, administrators, and policy makers serious about creating effective schools."

—*Chad Wick, Chairman, ACT, Inc., and founder and president emeritus, KnowledgeWorks*

"It takes a network. The desire to collaborate is innately human; true collaboration is responsible for our species' advancement. *Better Together* finally articulates the 'why' and 'how' collaboration via networking is the most exciting thing happening in education today."

—*Barry Schuler, Chairman, New Tech Network and partner, DFJ Growth*

"In *Better Together: How To Leverage School Networks for Smarter Personalized and Project Based Learning*, Tom Vander Ark and Lydia Dobyns convincingly demonstrate the power of school networks to transform learning so that all students develop the skills they need to be successful in college, career and life."

—David Ross, CEO,
Partnership for 21st Century Learning

"Tom Vander Ark and Lydia Dobyns understand that the future of education will be built on the shoulders of the strongest school networks. *Better Together* is a timely and much-needed book that advances a world of endless possibilities replete with practical and ready-to-use resources. The authors' unparalleled commitment to finding and highlighting over a hundred exemplar schools and networks that promote both inclusion and equity makes this book a must-read for all educators hoping to build a better world for the next generation of students and school leaders."

—Dr. Justin Aglio, Director of Academic Achievement and District Innovation, Montour School District

"*Better Together* makes the future of teaching and learning in a digital world understandable as well as less intimidating. Through the discussions of personalized learning and project based learning utilizing networks of learners and schools with teams focused on a common outcome, Tom and Lydia show us a future that is achievable.

They take the mystery out of the use of big data and artificial intelligence by showing us how to use school networks and our own agency to build a learning platform that is workable across America.

Hats off to the team for hitting it out of the park."

—Bev Perdue, Founder & Chair, digiLEARN 2015, Governor, State of North Carolina 2009–2013

"A decade's worth of organizing across hundreds of schools and organizations commonly committed to relevant, engaging, and equitable learning has made abundantly clear that our kids are much better off when their teachers, librarians, and youth workers as well as local artists, technologists, and entrepreneurs connect continuously. Networks make possible for diverse yet commonly-committed people to genuinely connect so that they imagine differently what's possible together. And then they're poised to forge ahead powerfully to remake learning."

—Gregg Behr, Executive Director at The Grable Foundation and Co-Chair of Remake Learning

"Vander Ark and Dobyns make incisive arguments about the power of networks for school innovation. For existing schools to iterate their way into the future, educators want to see and collaborate with others on the same path."

—Eileen Rudden, co-founder, LearnLaunch

"Engaging with our parents, teachers, principals, school board and students to seek their input to develop a district vision where all students graduate prepared for college or career paths is relatively easy. After all, we know what we want for our daughters and sons. The challenge is execution. School networks can make the difference in a district's ability to translate an active learner vision into reality. Vander Ark and Dobyns have depicted the success possible via network-district partnerships."

—*Juan Cabrera, Superintendent, El Paso*
Independent School District

BETTER
TOGETHER

BETTER TOGETHER

HOW TO LEVERAGE SCHOOL NETWORKS FOR SMARTER PERSONALIZED AND PROJECT BASED LEARNING

TOM VANDER ARK
LYDIA DOBYNS

JB JOSSEY-BASS™
A Wiley Brand

Published by Jossey-Bass
A Wiley Brand
One Montgomery Street, Suite 1000, San Francisco, CA 94104-4594—www.josseybass.com

Jossey-Bass books and products are available through most bookstores. To contact Jossey-Bass directly call our Customer Care Department within the U.S. at 800-956-7739, outside the U.S. at 317-572-3986, or fax 317-572-4002.

Wiley publishes in a variety of print and electronic formats and by print-on-demand. Some material included with standard print versions of this book may not be included in e-books or in print-on-demand. If this book refers to media such as a CD or DVD that is not included in the version you purchased, you may download this material at http://booksupport.wiley.com. For more information about Wiley products, visit www.wiley.com.

Library of Congress Cataloging-in-Publication Data

Names: Vander Ark, Tom, 1959- author. | Dobyns, Lydia, 1955- author.
Title: Better together : how to leverage school networks for smarter
    personalized and project based learning / by Tom Vander Ark, Lydia Dobyns.
Description: San Francisco, CA : Jossey-Bass ; Hoboken, NJ : John Wiley &
    Sons, 2018. | Includes index. |
Identifiers: LCCN 2018005474 (print) | LCCN 2018011283 (ebook) | ISBN
    9781119439523 (pdf) | ISBN 9781119439462 (epub) | ISBN 9781119439103 (cloth)
Subjects: LCSH: Communication in education. | Project method in teaching. |
    Educational innovations.
Classification: LCC LB1033.5 (ebook) | LCC LB1033.5 .V34 2018 (print) |
    DDC 371.102/2—dc23
LC record available at https://lccn.loc.gov/2018005474

Cover Design: Wiley
Cover Image: © DrAfter123/Getty Images

Printed in the United States of America
FIRST EDITION
HB Printing 10 9 8 7 6 5 4 3 2 1

CONTENTS

ABOUT THE AUTHORS

Tom Vander Ark advocates for innovation in learning. As CEO of Getting Smart, he advises schools and impact organizations on the path forward. Tom is the author of *Getting Smart, Smart Cities,* and *Smart Parents.* He previously served as the first Executive Director of Education for the Bill & Melinda Gates Foundation and as a public school superintendent in Washington State.

Lydia Dobyns has combined careers as a technology entrepreneur and executive with education policy and nonprofit service. Lydia is President and CEO of New Tech Network (NTN), a leading design partner for comprehensive school change. Starting with the first public district high school 20 years ago, New Tech Network consists of 200 K–12 schools in 28 states. NTN, a nonprofit organization, works with school districts to design innovative learning environments. Lydia previously served two terms as an elected school board member, co-founded and co-led a local education foundation, and directed replication strategies in the education sector. Her career includes work in the tech, online services, consumer products, and health care industries.

ACKNOWLEDGMENTS

We'd like to thank the teams we work with for their support and contributions to this project. The teachers, school directors, and district leaders who are the heartbeat of the New Tech Network are a constant source of inspiration and learning for us. The New Tech Network national team, dispersed across the country and anchored by the Napa office, demonstrate daily the potency of passion combined with the desire to get better. The Getting Smart team developed and supported the Network Effect blog series that led to this book.

For 20 years, we've worked and learned with school network leaders across America. We mentioned more than 75 networks and more than 50 school support organizations in this book (see the appendix) and have a learning relationship with almost every one of them. Their commitment to equity and excellence at scale has made an enormous contribution to innovating and improving American education. It is our hope that this book helps to acknowledge and advance their work.

PREFACE

We believe school networks are the most important invention of modern US education. We have worked with or sponsored most of the informal, voluntary, and managed school networks and believe that they, and the exciting new networks being developed, are the key to unlocking the power of new learning models—which are promising, but very difficult to develop and support.

Networks offer the best path forward to proven solutions, so that every school does not have to reinvent the wheel. Some offer the opportunity to innovate up from proven capabilities, as well as meaningful ways for educators to "give and get" expertise and create vibrant communities of adult learners. In addition, networks build sustainability by serving as a bridge during periods of leadership transition in school systems.

The dawn of an innovation age powered by the rise of artificial intelligence makes school networks more important than ever. For young people, the new era offers the opportunity to code an application, launch a campaign, solve big problems, or start a business. Emerging opportunities require young people to be skilled in attacking complex problems, working in diverse teams, and directing lifelong learning. While the new age comes with unprecedented opportunity, it will also be accompanied by massive waves of social change and unexpected challenges.

New learning models that combine personalized learning and extended team-based challenges help develop the knowledge, skills, and mindset necessary for success in the innovation age. But they remain complicated to design and implement, particularly for students with learning gaps and risk factors. This level of complexity reinforces the need to work together in networks of likeminded schools to meet new challenges.

Each of us started in business and saw the early stages of the technology revolution firsthand. Together, we helped create some of the first network businesses where it wasn't just scale economies (where stuff gets cheaper as you get bigger) that mattered—it was a network effect, where the customer experience got better as the network got bigger and smarter. This idea of working on platforms in networks has changed the world and continues to transform learning.

More than 20 years ago we both came to realize that education was the most important thing that we could work on, and that there was an emerging opportunity to transform learning and attack inequity. We imagined ways that platforms and networks could extend access and opportunity.

We share a passion for encouraging young people to take on the great challenges of our time—with the inspiration, support, examples, and time to do it well. In thousands of schools we have seen how extended and authentic challenges can help young people connect with their community and develop the cognitive muscles for difference-making.

We've seen some success and some failure in our public advocacy efforts to lead public school districts, nonprofit organizations, and philanthropic and venture investments. We've learned that good ideas are insufficient, and that transformation is hard to start and even harder to scale. This book is about the two conclusions we have reached, two ideas that can transform education: Powerful, project based learning, and taking it to scale by working together in networks.

It's not easy to create schools where every student is prepared to engage in powerful learning experiences, but it can be done, one school at a time. Networks of like-minded schools getting better together are the key. It's that dream that our work, and the work of our respective organizations, is all about. And it's why we're so passionate about this topic. We believe that, as expressed by the New Tech Network, we can create a nation proud of its public schools.

BETTER
TOGETHER

INTRODUCTION

The Promise of School Networks

Dan Leeser taught social studies in a traditional school district. He followed a scripted curriculum with a focus on preparing students for standardized tests. In 2015, Leeser had the opportunity to help launch a new high school that was part of a national network. Teachers in the network engage students in challenging, integrated projects. Leeser enjoys the creative work of designing his own projects using network tools. The inaugural class at Cougar New Tech created graphic novels that combined Greek myths with Asian culture—an interesting thought experiment that encouraged students to consider the role of myth in society in the past and the present.

Sarah Dominguez taught math in the same district, where the administration was fixated on test preparation. Sarah was frustrated by the lack of student engagement and the inability to reach students where they were and help them learn to collaborate. She jumped at the chance to join Leeser to start a new school focused on engaging learners in authentic challenges.

1

Dominguez selects some problems from the network library and creates others herself. Like Dan, Sarah appreciates the instructional coaching she receives and the annual network conference they attend.

Cougar New Tech opened as a new academy at Franklin High School in El Paso, Texas. It meets in its own facility and has the autonomy to use different tools, curriculum, and professional learning than the rest of the district. Cougar New Tech is one of eight academies in El Paso that belong to the New Tech Network. These small academies have a dual allegiance to the New Tech Network and the El Paso Independent School District. The district, pedagogically aligned with New Tech, allows the academies to use different schedules, courses, tools, and professional development experiences. As part of this network, Dan, Sarah, and the other Franklin Cougar teachers —most of whom are new to project based learning—benefit from a proven model, startup support, and on-site coaching, as well as a curriculum library, project authoring tools, and an annual conference.

For Sarah, being part of a network has provided her with the support and resources needed whenever she's struggling with an idea or a project. For example, when Sarah was feeling conflicted about how she wanted to teach calculus for the upcoming year, she was able to get connected with a teacher in another state and share ideas and feedback on how to approach calculus lessons and projects.

"Having a coherent model has allowed our students to know that we have high expectations across the board," said Sarah. "Students are comfortable and they know what to anticipate," Dan added, "because everybody is on board with the same ideologies and methods."

Franklin High School administrators were enthusiastic hosts of the new academy. Having visited similar schools, they knew it would be a high-quality learning option for some of their students. They appreciated the comprehensive nature of the school design, tools, and support, as well as having enough flexibility to make it their own.

New Tech Network is a network of voluntary association. Some of the 200 schools were newly created, like Cougar, and offered as schools of choice to students and teachers. School districts often opt to implement the New Tech model in existing schools as a school redesign initiative. Half of the schools in the network are neighborhood schools and the rest are schools of choice. For more than 15 years, public school districts around the country have looked to New Tech for support in promoting teaching that engages, a culture that empowers, technology that enables, and outcomes that matter.

WHY SCHOOL NETWORKS MATTER

School networks are the most important innovation in modern US education. Rather than layers of inherited features, schools that belong to networks are organized around a shared approach to teaching and learning, common tools, and collaborative learning opportunities for principals and classroom teachers.

Thousands of schools in traditional school districts voluntarily affiliate with organizations like the New Tech Network. Schools join the network, in part, because it works—more students are engaged, graduate, and go to college than in comparable schools.[1] School leaders cite similar reasons for joining Big Picture Learning, Expeditionary Learning (EL) Education, and the career-focused National Academy Foundation (NAF) network.

About a third of the 7,000 charter schools in the US operate in networks. Most are operated by nonprofit management organizations. A 2017 Stanford study showed that schools in strong networks outperformed unaffiliated schools.[2]

Curriculum networks provide programs of study on shared platforms with professional learning experiences. Project Lead The Way (PLTW) is a science, technology, engineering, and math (STEM) curriculum used by more than 10,000 schools that share a platform and training. The Advancement Via Individual Determination program, also known as AVID, is a college readiness system used by 6,000 schools that share structures, curriculum, and tools. These curriculum networks are not whole school models but they represent much deeper relationships than buying a textbook.

Why are we seeing a steady increase in schools working in networks? Why are they likely to become more important in the future? The primary reason, as previously cited, is that they work pretty well especially in difficult circumstances. Better than average performance is likely a function of a coherent design where everything works together for students and teachers. In many cases, commitment to common practices, tools, and training consistently produces better teaching.

Coherence and fidelity are becoming more important as teaching grows more complex. Using new tools to create personalized learning journeys for every student is promising but raises the degree of difficulty in education. New learning models require more tools, more collaboration, and more expertise. Working in a network that invests in a coherent model can help schools facing tough conditions achieve strong results.

What the William and Flora Hewlett Foundation calls deeper learning outcomes further adds to the level of challenge for individual schools. Building on the four key outcomes identified by the Partnership for 21st Century Skills—communication, critical thinking, collaboration, and creativity—deeper learning adds two additional outcomes: academic mindset, and learning how to learn. There is evidence that these outcomes are becoming more important for college and career readiness. US schools have struggled to achieve high standards in basic skills, and developing a new picture of what graduates should be able to do and identifying ways to promote and measure these new skills is challenging.

In addition to addressing the degree of difficulty problem, networks help create a sustained sense of focus that can help alleviate turnover. Almost all of these networks, both managed and voluntary, were formed by nonprofit organizations which have the benefit of perpetual rather than political leadership—and that allows them to create and sustain a mission-focused organization over a long period of time. A two-year study of innovation in education made apparent that sustained leadership was key to improved results.[3] Elected bodies like school boards have a difficult time sustaining an agenda. The average tenure of urban superintendents is about three years, and the average tenure for principals of high-challenge secondary schools is about the same.[4] Rapid leadership turnover is disastrous for sustained school improvement and creating an environment where innovation can flourish.

Because charter schools are authorized to operate outside district structures, they largely avoid the turmoil associated with waves of political change and rapid leadership turnover. School support organizations like the New Tech Network form district partnerships that result in new schools that often have charter-like autonomy through an agreement with the district. Purpose-designed schools often achieve early success and develop a constituency that also protects them from the consequences of turnover.

The last reason networks are likely to become more important is that they are organized to invest in improvement and innovation. School districts are usually cash-strapped from meeting current obligations, and not well organized to support investments that may take years to show a return. Networks offer coherent designs that support high fidelity teaching sustained over time and supported by investment.

WORKING IN NETWORKS

Networks typically have a hub that that organizes work and makes decisions. Some less formal networks, such as parent teacher organizations, self-organize and have multiple hubs. Networks may be spontaneous like Black Lives Matter, or planned and continuous like the NAACP. Networks may require a simple pledge or be as selective and expensive as the Augusta National Golf Club.

Networks usually support a core set of transactions that adds value for participants and the network as a whole. Millions of teachers work together in professional learning communities because they share a commitment to improving on shared practices. Schools in California joined the ConnectEd network to receive access to grant funding, technical assistance, a learning platform, and collaboration opportunities.[5] Foundations continue to fund managed school networks because they appear to be a reliable way to create quality schools in underserved communities.

This book is about steady increase in educators working together in networks—a trend we are confident will only continue to accelerate. An important part of this trend is that as dynamic networks with powerful platform tools create a network effect, they get better and more valuable as they grow—and in turn, the tools get better and the growth opportunities for staff members grow with scale. Along with many good examples highlighted in this book, the New Tech Network serves as an illustrative example of this network effect (which is discussed in greater detail in Chapter Two).

HOW NETWORKS LEVERAGE PLATFORMS

Digital platforms have transformed the way we live, work, travel and play—that is the thesis of Chapter One. However, despite the shift to digital learning, the platform revolution has yet to fully transform formal education. So what's the hold up?

The first problem is that learning platforms have not received the same level of attention and investment as social media and marketplace platforms; they are generally still a few years behind what we have all come to expect in user experience. More importantly, after adding more than 30 million computers to US schools, it has become clear that it is not technology tools that transform learning, but rather a vision of powerful learner experiences made possible by new tools and environments. Learning is also transformed by new working conditions for teachers to construct experiences that impact thousands and, simultaneously, enable small group instruction. It is a professional work environment for classroom educators and school leaders that supports multiple contributions and provides personalized professional growth opportunities.

Project based learning is easy to initiate but hard to do rigorously. Adding personalized learning, where every learner has a unique path and pace, is promising but complicated. It remains academically, technically, and financially challenging to construct a personalized learning model, a learning platform, and an aligned professional learning system.

The situation is further complicated in US public schools by a decentralized system where 14,000 superintendents and school boards operating in 50 very different state contexts are charged with designing and operating instructional programs. Managed and voluntary networks can develop the scale to invest in an instructional programs, technology platforms, improvement frameworks, and professional learning opportunities.

We wrote this book because we are excited about the potential of new learning models to dramatically improve achievement and extend access. However, the work is complicated and difficult. Educators should work in networks, or in districts that act like networks in order to get better.

USING THIS BOOK

The first section (Chapter One to Chapter Three) provides some background on the technology revolution underway and how and why platforms and networks are reshaping life and work. The second section (Chapter Four through Chapter Eight) describes our vision of powerful learning for all students and why design thinking is the new framework for school. Chapter Six describes the empowered environment of co-creation that teachers should expect. Chapter Seven describes how dynamic networks improve. Chapter Eight compares network models for scaled impact.

The third section of the book contains specific strategies you can use to build an impactful network including leadership (Chapter Nine), business models (Chapter Ten), governance (Chapter Eleven), school support (Chapter Twelve), and advocacy (Chapter Thirteen).

NOTES

1. https://32dkl02ezpk0qcqvqmlx19lk-wpengine.netdna-ssl.com/wp-content/uploads/2016/08/2016annualdatareportfinalspreadssm.pdf
2. https://credo.stanford.edu/pdfs/CMO%20FINAL.pdf
3. http://gettingsmart.com/publication/smartcities
4. https://www.cgcs.org/cms/lib/DC00001581/Centricity/Domain/87/Urban%20Indicator_Superintendent%20Summary%2011514.pdf
5. http://www.gettingsmart.com/2017/06/connected-takes-linked-learning-national

PART ONE

PLATFORM REVOLUTION

PLATFORMS

A Place You Call Home

Push a button and soon a car shows up wherever you are. Search, click on your favorite dish, and a few minutes later dinner arrives. Want to make a quick trip to New York? A flight and a room in a stranger's apartment are a few clicks away. Perhaps you'll visit your friend from high school—you can tell from your Facebook feed that he's enjoying his new grandkids.

Digital platforms have transformed the way we live, work, play, travel, and learn. The six largest firms (by market capitalization[1])—Apple, Alibaba, Alphabet, Amazon, Facebook, and Microsoft—all run platform businesses. Academics Geoffrey

Parker, Marshall Van Alstyne and Sangeet Choudary explore the *Platform Revolution* in their 2016 book. They define a platform this way:

> A platform is a business based on enabling value-creating interactions between external producers and consumers. The platform provides an open, participative infrastructure for these interactions and sets governance conditions for them. The platform's overarching purpose: to consummate matches among users and facilitate the exchange of goods, services or social currency, thereby enabling value creation for all participants.[2]

Platforms like Uber, Airbnb, Facebook, Amazon, and Alibaba have transformed consumer options and markets, but most of us don't know much about how they work. A handful of design decisions about governance, openness, and monetization guide user experience and can make the difference between scale and obscurity. For example, MySpace required users to visit other people's content while Facebook brought friend's content to the user's feed—and this small design decision made all the difference.

The rise of the platform economy and lifestyle has been supported by improved access to broadband and a dozen trends (as summarized in the accompanying grid of what platforms do and enable), which has created accelerating and unceasing change unlike anything before. Platforms change assumptions about what is possible, and they unlock new sources of value creation and supply. LinkedIn is where we connect for business. Facebook is home for friends and family. Snapchat is where we share pictures. Amazon is where we buy everything. These platforms enable new and important activities.

What platforms do	What platforms enable
Thin services (like Slack) are fast, extensible, interoperable, and easy to learn	**Move** freely with fluid information linked across all of your screens to learn, work, and transact anywhere
Know your preferences, locations, competencies, and interests	**Connect** on interests, events, and campaigns; build collective solutions
Filter the flow of information and allocate attention to the exponentially expanding universe	**Create** compelling images, stories, campaigns, tools, environments, and experiences. Platforms eliminate gatekeepers and scale efficiently.
Track everything and share it in simple, useful visuals	**Mix and match** playlists and new compilations
Recommend and remind with increasing accuracy and usefulness	**Share** public products with broad audiences, create community feedback loops, and bring the outside in
Improve seamlessly and continuously (no more monolithic versioning)	**Learn** and grow between face-to-face interactions

You probably work on several platforms. Any form of marketing starts with knowing your customers—and potential customers. Information about them is stored in a Customer Relationship Management system like Salesforce. If your company makes something, it probably uses Enterprise Resource Planning software to manage production and inventory. Human resources and accounting also usually have their own software. Over the last decade, all of these systems have migrated from operating on a computer at the business level, to operating over the Internet "in the cloud," which makes it easy to access anywhere, easy to update, and easy to scale with growth.

Just when it looked like these giant platforms would do everything, smartphones came around. Shortly after the introduction of the iPhone in 2007, a new kind of platform was born—and the Apple App Store quickly became a home for thousands, and now millions, of mobile applications. Hundreds of billions of mobile apps have been downloaded from the App Store, Google Play, and Windows Phone Store. What was once a phone is now a mobile computing platform.

With the growth in smartphone penetration and social media use came text messaging. It exploded with young people. And then Baby Boomers with email inboxes full of spam figured out that texting was much easier than email for many conversations. Slack, launched in 2014, quickly became a unicorn (valued at more than $1 billion). Millions of companies quickly adopted the thin messaging platform, which was easy to integrate. Slack proved that you don't have to be monolithic, you just have to solve a problem and be easy to use.

Platforms help us create, often co-create, and connect with broader audiences. Platforms learn about us and help us learn about the world. For most of us, growth is activated by relationships, and learning happens in community settings (more on learning platforms in Chapter Three). Platforms can make face-to-face time more productive and can provide engagement in the gap between in-person experiences.

PLATFORM ARMS RACE

Technology platforms shift every 10 to 15 years. The personal computer was the platform for a decade beginning in 1985, until the internet exploded on the scene as the new platform in 1994. The smartphone was introduced in 2007. With each shift, it appears that disproportionate gains go to the leader in the new domain. It looks like the new battlefield is artificial intelligence and augmented and virtual reality. The six big platform companies spend $50 billion a year on research and development, and a sizeable portion will go to these emerging capabilities.[3]

Vibrant platforms incorporate new user interfaces that enable new functionality and create new geographic freedom. More than 150 million Snapchat users watch 20 billion videos daily, with users spending almost a half an hour on the platform every day. Facebook bought Oculus betting that the next interface would be virtual reality. With Alexa, Amazon bet on voice as the new interface. In the coming months, digital assistants and chatbots will become more widespread thanks to advances in artificial intelligence. Speech recognition will continue to improve and will power a variety of interaction-based services.

How do platforms scale and unlock value? The secret is network effects.

NOTES

1. http://dogsofthedow.com/largest-companies-by-market-cap.htm
2. Geoffrey G. Parker, Marshall W. Van Alstyne, and Sangeet Paul Choudary (2016). *Platform Revolution: How Networked Markets Are Transforming the Economy and How to Make Them Work for You.* New York, NY: W.W. Norton & Company.
3. https://techcrunch.com/2017/06/02/how-to-create-the-most-value-for-the-next-technology-wave

NETWORK EFFECTS
When Bigger Is Better

As businesses grow, there are often negative consequences to customers, employees, and even the company itself. But when networks grow, there are many ways members can benefit. If Walmart gets a new customer, your benefit is negligible. When Facebook gets a new member, each of us has someone new to connect with or learn from—and the platform gets bigger and potentially better with each new user. Online gamers benefit from participation of other gamers. Both are examples of positive network effects—each new addition makes the platform better.

Large, well-managed platform communities produce significant value for each user. Value can be driven by the power of social networks (*can I connect, contribute, and get what I need?*), demand aggregation (*can I buy things?*), and application development (*can I build things?*).

Platforms promote exchanges of information, goods and services, and some form of currency. The ability to monetize that value exchange in some way is key to building a scalable and sustainable platform. Platforms are in the curation business; they match content and connections at scale. Most platforms use an algorithmic filter to screen out or deprioritize less valuable content. Filters and recommendations can help match participants with units of value.

"Network effects turn organizations inside out," claim the authors of *Platform Revolution*. That means users run the place. Platforms are like information factories that have no control over inventory. They just attract and match to facilitate value exchanges.

NETWORKS ARE BIG BUSINESS

A Wharton study of 1,500 organizations (using machine learning to scour big data sets) found four primary business models[1]:

- *Asset builders*. Manufacturers, distributors, and retailers (WalMart, Ford, FedEx)
- *Technology creators*. Biotech, healthtech and fintech (Microsoft, Oracle, Amgen)
- *Service providers*. Consultants, bankers, educators, and lawyers (Aetna, JP Morgan, Accenture)
- *Network orchestrators*. Social, business and financial (TripAdvisor, RedHat, Uber)

The study found that networks, on average, yield the highest growth, margins, and returns. According to study leader Barry Libert, "Network Orchestrators, which leverage intangible assets, and real time interactions, apply to all organizations regardless of industry."

Compared to asset builders that make things, service providers who sell hours, and tech providers who sell intellectual property, the study found a large performance differential for networks, which the authors called a *Multiplier Effect*, owing to the rules of network versus firm centric business models.

Networks bring people together (often called a two-sided revenue model) like credit cards (cardholders and merchants), operating systems (users and developers), recruitment sites (job seekers and recruiters), and marketplaces (buyers and sellers).

Networks often leverage co-creation and network assets (like cars, houses, friends, and insights) to perform better financially than organizations that sell hours or make stuff.

Network leaders even think and talk differently; they use words like platform, network, digital, and mobile to describe their firms and investment strategies, whereas "Asset Builder" leaders talk about plants, property, and equipment as their primary focus and investments.

When a school district gets bigger, it means more headaches —the organization does not necessarily get smarter. But when a personal learning network grows, there's a good chance it can get smarter, because it becomes more likely that another educator faced similar situations. And you gain access to hundreds of resources rather than dozens. When schools join the New Tech Network, teachers gain access to a library of projects they can adopt or adapt. When schools join the Summit Learning network, students gain access to tailored digital playlists, and Summit gains insight into what resources work best.

Large platform networks can continuously run a series of randomized controlled trials with the goal of finding out what interventions really make a difference to student success, improving the outcomes or the efficiency of learning or both.[2] Bror Saxberg, who works with the Chan Zuckerberg Initiative (the technology partner for Summit Learning), calls this platform-enabled design work "learning engineering." It is all about using data to improve the learner and staff experience— and the more data you have, the smarter the system gets.

CAPS NETWORK

Launched in 2009 with 100 students, The Center for Advanced Professional Studies (CAPS) created professional-based learning opportunities for 100 pioneering students. Formed by the Blue Valley School District southwest of Kansas City, the high school career center now serves more than 1,000 Blue Valley students each year. CAPS anchors a network of 74 school districts across 12 states serving 10,000 students. Partner schools commit to five core values:

Profession-Based Learning. Instructors develop real-world, project-based learning strategies through collaborations with business and community partners. These interactions enhance the learning experience, providing students with college and career preparation.

Professional Skills Development. Unique experiences allow students to cultivate transformative, professional skills such as understanding expectations, time management, and other essential business values. These skills are critical to providing students with a competitive advantage in their postsecondary education and professional careers.

Self-Discovery and Exploration. Students realize their strengths and passions by exploring and experiencing potential professions. This allows them to make informed decisions about their future, while learning to exhibit leadership in the process.

Entrepreneurial Mindset. Instructors create an environment where creative thinking and problem-solving is encouraged. An innovative culture is key to fostering entrepreneurial learning and design thinking.

Responsiveness. CAPS supports high-skill, high-demand careers through ongoing innovation in curriculum development, programs, and services based on local business and community needs.

CAPS director Corey Mohn finds three keys to network success: relationship building, a high level of trust between stakeholders, and value creation from affiliation. "When members use the network, it's like exercise," explains Mohn, "and the connective tissue gets stronger."[3]

Scaling up success in any organization or educational institution is difficult, but networks can make it much easier. "We view scale as positive," explains Phil Regier, Dean for Educational Initiatives at Arizona State University (ASU). "We're going to use scale to get better. Digital learning tends to be scale games. As you get bigger, you can make the technology better."[4]

Regier uses the Global Freshman Academy, an online learning partnership with edX, as an example of network effects. It allows learners to take open classes anytime and only pay after passing a class. "The math class is fantastic, and the bigger it gets, the better it gets," said Regier. That's because the adaptive courseware adjusts to each learner and collects thousands of data points that create a greater network effect.

Why is bigger better? More data helps ASU determine which learning experiences are most productive. It helps design more productive pathways by predicting what kinds of help each type of learner will need. "If we have 2,000 students we can improve faster than if 150 students take a course," added Regier. "The more students I have taking an adaptive course, the better the course will be, the faster and more efficiently students will learn—and learn more skills more deeply."

By leveraging digital learning, Regier sees the emergence of several very large institutions, what president Michael Crow calls national service universities, that can serve more than 200,000 learners. Through programs like the Global Freshman Academy and ASU partnership serving Starbucks employees, Crow has his sights set on being a super scalable university—a big platform network.[5]

Impact organizations, as well as mission-driven nonprofit and for-profit organizations, increasingly leverage networks. A few rely on advertisements or sponsorships. Everfi has grown a big business by developing and distributing sponsored curriculum. Some impact organizations provide free services—access to a platform or open education resources (OER)—and sell additional services to boot. EL Education and Open Up Resources offer training around free math and English curriculum. Most education networks are membership or subscription supported.

A handful of organizations rely entirely on philanthropic support for the development of impact networks. They range from voluntary pledge networks like FutureReady to 10 schools that received $10 million monster grants from XQ: The Super School Project sponsored by philanthropist Laurene Powell Jobs.

Some network business models shown in the following table look a lot like an open marketplace, but there are three key differences. First, networks require an affirmative decision to associate. Second, network members gain access to network resources (brand, services, information sources, premium content). And finally, networks create interdependence between members by rewarding transactions that create mutual value. (Network business models are discussed in further detail in Chapter Ten.)

NETWORK BUSINESS MODELS

Engine	Business Examples	Education Examples
Ads/Sponsored Freemium	Facebook LinkedIn	Everfi • OER and Professional Learning: EL Education, Open Up Resources • Services: Edmodo
Membership, Subscription	Bar associations, chambers of commerce	• Individuals: National Education Association (NEA), The School Superintendents Association (AASA) • Curriculum: AVID, PLTW • Schools: New Tech Network, Big Picture
Platform Markets	Uber, Airbnb	Udemy, CottageClass, TeachersPayTeachers,
Impact	Wikipedia	FutureReady, Summit Learning, NGLC, XQ, YouthBuild

STRUCTURES DRIVE BEHAVIOR

If you drove west from Houston to Los Angeles on I-10, El Paso Texas would mark the halfway point. It's 300 miles west of what east Texans call "West Texas." El Paso and Juarez Mexico straddle the Rio Grande and wrap around the 7,000 foot peaks of the Franklin Mountains, the southernmost point of the Rocky Mountains. With Las Cruces, New Mexico, the metroplex is home to almost three million people and is the largest bilingual and binational workforce in the Americas, and perhaps the world.

Two miles east of the bustling downtown is Chamizal, the hardscrabble neighborhood where artist Mauricio Olague grew up. He uses the physical discards of this working class Mexican-American community to create "aggressive, streetwise works" that "protect humanity's spiritual essence" through "objects tied to a specific time and space."[6]

Like his art, Olague is tied to this place. He attended Bowie High, which backs up to the border, and then the University of Texas at El Paso. He returned to Bowie as a teacher and watched his district become more and more obsessed with standardized tests. In many classes, the curriculum was built around released state test items. This obsession with test preparation lead to cheating and manipulating results to earn bonuses. In 2012, Superintendent Lorenzo García was convicted of fraud and sentenced to six years in jail.

The state took control of the district and appointed a board of managers who, under the leadership of Superintendent Juan Cabrera, began shifting away from a focus on preparing for tests to active learning—a combination of personalized, project-based, and social emotional learning with a strong commitment to dual language. Cabrera invited the New Tech

Network to help develop project-based academies in eight El Paso neighborhoods.

After two decades of teaching and service as a community artist, Olague reluctantly joined a project to form a new academy at Bowie High which serves 1,400 Hispanic students, nearly all of whom live in or near poverty and learned Spanish as their first language.

While skeptical at first, Olague liked the idea of teaching integrated projects. He became a founding Oso New Tech teacher at Bowie High, where he currently leads a unique art and biology mash-up and has grown to love the challenge of team teaching. As a lifelong resident of the neighborhood, he sees this high engagement approach as a great way to motivate students and prepare them for what lies ahead. "We are the new thing; we are what's happening; we have school reform happening right now. We can make a difference," said Olague. "This is the tool to fix the problem."[7]

Diego Medina, another founding Oso New Tech teacher, teaches English in a course that includes World History. He loves the opportunity to incorporate literature into history and study the geography of historical texts. These veteran teachers share a completely new context—big, integrated team-taught blocks, in a national network full of like-minded teachers, and in a district that values whole-child learning.

Mauricio and Diego work in a generative environment that values collaboration and creativity—a small team that is part of a big network, and a structure that encourages and supports positive behavior in teachers and students. Just a year before, there was a sense of scripted helplessness serving the high-need student population. For Mauricio and Diego, Oso New Tech represents a big break with the past: new goals and expectations, a small personalized environment, different and shared pedagogical approach, and new collaborative teaching roles and assessment strategies, all supported by common platform tools and yielding sustained student engagement.

The formation of Oso New Tech demonstrates that the same people in a different structure with a different connections completely changes the group dynamic.[8] Management guru Edward Deming said, "A bad system will beat a good person every time."[9] New Tech and similar networks suggests the flip side is also true—a good system helps good people achieve great things.

For 20 years, US education has focused myopically on individual test results. For even longer US businesses have focused on individual performance reviews. The success of networks in business and education suggests that "the first role of a leader is as system architect—getting the conditions, connections, and culture right," said author and advisor Niels Pflaeging. "Work on the system, not the people," he added, stressing that "Leadership has to be work focused on improving the system."[10]

REMAKE LEARNING: A LOCAL LEARNING NETWORK

Pittsburgh has a legacy of making things, from steel to computer algorithms. When Gregg Behr, executive director of The Grable Foundation, thought about inventing the future of learning in the Greater Pittsburgh Region, he decided not to import national school networks but build on local strengths. Behr and colleagues built Remake Learning, a regional network of more than 250 schools, universities, libraries, startups, nonprofits, and museums to provide children and families with equitable access to relevant, meaningful learning experiences that leverage technology, art, the learning sciences, and diverse environments.

For a decade, the Remake Learning collaborative has worked to supercharge the region's social sector on behalf of kids. "We believe that in order to truly prepare kids for tomorrow, we need to equip them not only with deep content knowledge and high-tech tools, but also the skills, creativity, and empathy necessary for building a more com-passionate, sustainable world," said Behr.

The Grable, MacArthur, and Pittsburgh foundations, as well as others, have invested more than $55 million to advance innovative education across greater Pittsburgh. Their signa-ture event is Remake Learning Days, a spring festival billed as the world's largest open house for teaching and learning.

The Sprout Fund, which manages the network, docu-mented the formula for spreading project-based, real-world learning opportunities in the *Remake Learning Playbook*, the recipe for a learning innovation ecosystem.

TRUST ECOSYSTEMS

In the 1990s, Barry Schuler spotted the rise of interactive media, computing power, graphics, and hyperlinking and built a company that combined these tools. That company, Meteor, was sold to America Online (AOL) and Schuler went on to help turn AOL into a media powerhouse. Schuler, now the board chair of the New Tech Network, said networks didn't come along with the Internet: "Philosophically, they are the oldest idea in the world, manifest as religion." We don't usu-ally think of religion as a network, but for thousands of years religion served as a platform of beliefs, gathering places, and collaboration. Religions were the first trust platform for a perplexing world.[11]

There are many examples of trust ecosystems in the modern internet economy. With broadband and a connected, "We see network effects firing up worldwide," said Schuler. After landing at an unfamiliar airport, you tap a button on your phone, walk to a designated spot, and a person you have never met picks you up and takes you to a designated location. The driver has seen your rating and is confident that you will be neat and polite and that he will get paid. And you in turn trust in his five-star rating. After a hundred rides it still seems magical—affordable convenient transportation supported by a trust transaction on Lyft or Uber. Online marketplaces like eBay, Amazon, and Alibaba facilitate trillions of dollars of retail transactions each year by facilitating trust between buyers and sellers through rating systems and consistent delivery.

Heard of the digital currency Bitcoin? It is based on Blockchain, an open-source distributed ledger system that facilitates collaboration and tracking of all kinds of transactions and interactions. Rather than being held by an information middlemen, like a bank manager, Blockchain distributes a record of transactions to every party that is interested. It creates a trust protocol that enables commercial transactions without a third party. New services that incorporate Blockchain will transform financial services, music, and education.[12]

In education today, transcripts are the crude currency of learning—a simple record of courses and credits culminating in degrees. But increasingly credentials, smaller skill demonstrations called microcredentials, and other artifacts of learning are being shared in digital portfolios and on professional profiles including LinkedIn. With the shift from print-based to digital learning, the amount of data about each learner is exploding. But learners lack a systematic way to share a record of what they know and can do. Educational institutions and hiring entities don't have a common way to verify learning experiences and demonstrations. Platforms that incorporate trust protocols like Blockchain will change that in the next few years, making it as easy a few clicks to verify a learning journey and an applicant's demonstrated capacities.

Blockchain will not only improve the trustworthiness of credential data, it will improve security. With copies of the blockchain distributed in many places rather than one central location, it is essentially tamper-proof—hack one node and tens of thousands of nodes will reject the manipulated records. A number of new applications are used to secure health and financial data; as more education data is transferred using Blockchain, similar applications will be used to prevent identity theft.

While platforms have added convenience and connection to our lives, and transactions have become more secure, there can still be unintended consequences. The proliferation of "fake news" on social media networks is one such consequence. Platforms armed with artificial intelligence have learned each of our preferences, and serve up more of the news and stories we want to see. As a result, we live in information gullies driven by curated interests and algorithms, making it less likely that we get "the rest of the story," as radio host Paul Harvey used to say. Platform operators are scrambling to add truth algorithms to address the fake news problem. This cautionary tale suggests that constant vigilance will be required to avoid algorithmic blindness and unintended bias while maintaining a balanced perspective.

DYNAMIC NETWORKS

There's not one version of Facebook. "At any point in time there are probably 10,000 versions," said CEO Mark Zuckerberg. "Any engineer can test something with 10,000 or 50,000 people, whatever is necessary to get a good test. Then, they get a readout of all of the metrics we care about: how are people connecting and sharing, do people have more friends, does it improve efficiency?" If it worked, the engineer takes the idea to a manager for incorporating in the base code. If not, they add it to the documentation of failed trials.

With a user base approaching two billion users, Facebook remains a dynamic network where Zuckerberg says the goal is to "Learn as quickly as possible what our community wants us to do."[13] Three things enable Facebook's strategy of learn and go as fast as you can: a culture that encourages people to try things; infrastructure that allows people to do just that (i.e., run 10,000 versions simultaneously); and a testing framework that helps determine how well the trial worked.

LEARNING TO LEAD A NETWORK

As Commander of US Forces in Afghanistan, Stanley McChrystal quickly recognized that the opposition was more like a network than an army. He realized "that to defeat a networked enemy we had to become a network ourselves. We had to figure out a way to retain our traditional capabilities of professionalism, technology, and, when needed, overwhelming force, while achieving levels of knowledge, speed, precision, and unity of effort that only a network could provide."

"As we learned to build an effective network," McChrystal concluded, "We also learned that leading that network—a diverse collection of organizations, personalities, and cultures—is a daunting challenge in itself. That struggle remains a vital, untold chapter of the history of a global conflict that is still underway."[14]

Most school networks don't share those three characteristics. For example, Job Corps is an education and job training program run by the Department of Labor that serves 60,000 youths, ages 16–24, in 125 centers across the country (about 70% of which are managed by contractors). This well-intentioned $1.7 billion program costs over $25,000 per student. It claims to be "a holistic career development training approach" but the sites we've seen are depressing places where congressional regulations stifle innovations—the opposite of an adaptive, emergent, and dynamic network. There are thousands of great teachers in Job Corp, but they are trapped in a compliance-oriented system lacking the culture, infrastructure, and data dashboard that drives networked platforms like Facebook forward.

Despite the fact that the Common Core Standards movement "sucked a lot of the innovation oxygen over last few years," as one leading impact investor put it, in the last few years leading school networks have moved forward with many new projects. Let's acknowledge that tech startups by nature are more dynamic than the more regulated public education environments—and for good reason: safety, privacy, and equity are all important considerations. But there are a growing number of school networks trying to operate more like Facebook than Job Corp. They provide four lessons about dynamic networks.

Dynamic networks learn bottom up. Learning Assembly is a network of seven school support organizations supported by the Bill & Melinda Gates Foundation. The network shares methods and infrastructure for piloting innovative teaching practices and tools. A network toolkit allows classroom teachers to support pilots from pilot planning, to supporting implementation, and reporting results. Through the 2016–2017 school year, the network has applied and tested 100 tools in 195 schools.

Because teachers in the New Tech Network are able to author or adapt projects, the network innovates from the bottom up with a growing library of curriculum units. Mauricio Olague (the Oso New Tech art teacher discussed earlier in this chapter) may be the only art teacher in America teaching an integrated course with Biology. The projects he constructs are unique contributions to the network—and the field.

Learn outside in. Smart networks take every opportunity to learn from developments outside the network. Harmony Public Schools, a Texas network of 54 schools, used a large federal grant to add project-based learning to their STEM-focused personalized learning model.

In Milwaukee, Carmen Schools of Science and Technology added career and technical education to their college preparation program.

In a lowly portable classroom just south of the Los Angeles airport, Da Vinci Schools piloted a blended and personalized learning model serving transient and foster students. The proposal was one of ten that won a $10 million XQ grant.

Update infrastructure. IDEA, a large Texas school network added blended learning to its high performing K–12 school model. Like Match Education in Boston, IDEA is experimenting with College for America (an innovative program of Southern New Hampshire University) to expand postsecondary opportunities for their students.

After waves of local innovations in personalized learning, the national Knowledge Is for Power Program (or KIPP network) is encouraging use of a digital platform to extend the benefits of a core curriculum and character development resources. KIPP also connects with and supports graduates as they enroll, attend, and complete college.

New Tech Network updated Echo, their project-based learning platform, to allow 5,000 K–12 teachers to share project-based lessons, classroom resources, and support individual professional development through earning badges and collective learning experiences across the network.

Share generously. Dynamic networks encourage and reward contribution inside and outside the network. Success Academies built a big school network that helped low income New York City students outperform kids from the suburbs and shared the formula with the world through an Education Institute which provides open access to the architecture and components of the successful model.

Summit Public Schools is a network of 14 innovative west coast secondary schools. Their learning platform, now supported by the Chan Zuckerberg Initiative, is shared with more than 100 teacher teams around the country that applied to a program called Summit Learning.

These dynamic networks value contributions over control, place an emphasis on transparency, and are generous and proactive about sharing lessons and capacity.

NOTES

1. https://news.wharton.upenn.edu/press-releases/2016/06/
networks-and-platform-based-business-models-win-in-the-digital-age-
according-to-a-new-study-by-the-wharton-school-of-the-university-
of-pennsylvanias-sei-center-for-advanced-studies-in-m
2. http://www.gettingsmart.com/2016/07/learning-engineering-making-
its-way-in-the-world
3. http://www.gettingsmart.com/2017/08/activating-a-network-
relationships-trust-and-being-selfish
4. http://postsecondary.gatesfoundation.org/podcast/episode-5-voices-
asugsv-expanding-opportunity
5. http://www.gettingsmart.com/2017/05/michael-crow-on-whats-next-
in-highered-and-the-edtech-tools-it-will-take
6. http://latinoartcommunity.org/community/ChicArt/ArtistDir/
MauOla.html
7. http://www.gettingsmart.com/2017/05/transforming-border-learning-
experiences-new-tech-network-in-el-paso
8. https://www.ted.com/talks/nicholas_christakis_the_hidden
_influence_of_social_networks/transcript?language=en
9. https://blog.deming.org/2015/02/a-bad-system-will-beat-a-good-
person-every-time
10. http://interactioninstitute.org/organize-for-complexity
11. http://www.gettingsmart.com/2017/06/getting-smart-podcast-barry-
schuler-on-the-power-of-networks
12. Don Tapscott, Alex Tapscott, and Jeff Cummings (2016). *Blockchain
Revolution: How the Technology Behind Bitcoin Is Changing Money, Business, and the World.* New York, NY: Portfolio.
13. https://mastersofscale.com/mark-zuckerberg-imperfect-is-perfect/
14. http://foreignpolicy.com/2011/02/21/it-takes-a-network

LEARNING PLATFORMS

When Will They Transform Education?

In 1994, Paul Wezeman was one of the founding teachers at Enterprise Elementary (and yes, the Seattle area school is named after the Star Trek starship). With a computer for every two students and "WWW" on the cover of *Time* magazine, Paul understood that the challenge in his project-based fifth grade classroom had just shifted from information scarcity to information abundance. For a project on ancient Egypt, the challenge flipped from scouring the library for a few books on Egypt to sorting and synthesizing online resources. Paul's insight transformed his classroom and inspired his superintendent.

Wezeman's classroom inspired the question, "Could a school operate on the Internet?" Tom visited Mike Feuling's fifth-grade classroom at nearby Adelaide Elementary School and described the benefits of a school that, compared to lectures and textbooks, changed how and when students learned. Tom explained that a great math teacher like Mike could reach thousands of students and still facilitate a one-on-one session with a student across the state. "Because the students can progress at their own speed, the Internet school will serve students who are ahead and those that are behind," explained Tom.

Shortly after those first platform daydreams, the Internet Academy was formed and Feuling was one of two brave founding teachers. After a year of operating as an online high school for Washington State students, the Internet Academy added elementary grades and became the first K–12 online public school in the country. Twenty years later, Mike is still lead teacher and curriculum director at the Internet Academy where he has supported a generation of full and part-time online learners.

A dozen local, regional, and national competitors have joined the Internet Academy in serving Washington State. Together, they reach a small percentage of students. Yet in aggregate, rather than transforming learning, these online schools have been criticized for being ineffective for many students.

What went wrong? As technology optimists, we have been pondering disappointing online learning results (and, as discussed below, weak technology integration results) for two decades. It comes down to weak tools, strong constraints, and human nature.

The first problem with online learning is that the platforms are not very good—they often lag behind social media developments by five years. Most online content is not much better than digitized textbooks, and most assessments are multiple choice. While *Getting Smart* predicted that learning platforms would boost customization, motivation, and equalization, they just have not done a great job on any of those fronts yet (but more on that later!).

The second problem with online learning is that deployment remains confined by tradition and policy constraints: an agrarian calendar, discipline-based courses, and age cohorts in lockstep synchronous classes. In many states, high-challenge students receive less funding and resources, and online charter schools are often underfunded in comparison to traditional schools. A unique problem that plagues online charter schools is that their well-intentioned authorization prohibits them from screening for likelihood of success in an online environment, which in turn prevents an adequate orientation (as the laws that produce these provider behaviors are intended to prevent the screening out of less capable students).

Here is what online success and failure looks like in practice. Jose is in middle school and has moved twice with his mother. After falling further behind with each move, he entered a new high school two and three years behind in literacy and math, respectively. He was bullied by fellow classmates, and hated school. Four weeks into the year, his mother enrolled him in an online school (which is quite typical in terms of enrollment, as many national online learning providers report that a significant majority of students enroll late and enter well behind). Due to his later enrollment, Jose did not receive the benefits of an interview to discuss the demands of learning online and the conditions necessary for success. Jose found success in math because he liked moving at his own pace, and was able to make up two years. Despite this progress, he still tested a year below grade level in the spring—and the state accountability system values proficiency more than growth. English literacy also proved to be a continuing challenge. Jose just doesn't like to read and never engaged in his previous English classes. Despite some online outreach, he failed the self-paced online class and now tests three years behind in reading and writing. The school receives a failing grade on the state accountability system despite a significant contribution in math. Jose moves again and goes to a new high school, and the online school is penalized for having a low graduation rate.

The third challenge with online learning is that for most human beings, learning is activated by relationships—growth happens in community. A few people will plow through a physics textbook or an online class just because they love the subject, but for most students, a teacher has a lot to do with the level of motivation and engagement. When online classes are successful, you often hear students describe strong personal relationships with their teacher as the reason. An online student like Jose needed an advocate at school to monitor his progress and help problem-solve his lack of engagement—the kind of thing that happens at good schools, online or traditional, but it is harder to do at a distance.

These days, most students in American schools have access to technology. The rapid adoption of inexpensive Google Chromebooks helped plunge the ratio to a computer for every two students. Most secondary schools have at least partial adoption of a learning platform—either a top-down district or network platform subscription decision, or various teacher adoptions of free platforms. And despite progress in online access, technology deployments have typically failed to live up to expectations.

Why has technology failed to transform education? Most of the shortcomings of online learning apply more broadly to all of elementary and secondary education. But let's start with the first reason—the tools just are not very good yet.

WHY ARE LEARNING PLATFORMS STILL SO BAD?

Millennials fondly recall playing Oregon Trail and Incredible Machines—engaging video computer games purchased in shrink-wrapped boxes of floppy disks in the 1980s and 1990s. The rise of free games on the Internet in the late 1990s followed by the dot com bust of 2001 largely killed off investment in learning games.

With all the education technology (EdTech) headlines these days, it is easy to forget that there was no venture investment in the sector 10 years ago; in fact, there were no EdTech venture funds until the end of 2008. Textbook publishers were beginning to make some digital investments, but there were few startups in the EdTech landscape. Education lagged well behind exploding investment in consumer internet, enterprise tools, and biotechnology.

From 2008 to 2018, EdTech venture spending increased from almost nothing to $3 billion of annual global investment in learning startups (and $1 billion of that in the US). That sounds like a lot, but it is a $5 trillion sector.[1] Healthcare venture investing in the US alone topped $7 billion in 2017.[2]

Platforms including Coursera, edX, Skillshare, and Udemy have transformed informal learning and career education. Wikipedia and YouTube have made it possible for anyone to learn almost anything. More people are using Duolingo to learn a language than all the high school students in the US.

Most higher education institutions have adopted a learning management systems (LMS). Blackboard, Canvas (Instructure), Brightspace (D2L), and Moodle account for more than 80% of the LMS market.[3] Such adoptions may have boosted efficacy and perhaps efficiency, but most have been well short of transformational. LMS adoptions have not dramatically changed price, access to, or quality of higher education in the long run.

LMS have lower penetration in K–12 (particularly elementary), but lightweight tools like Edmodo and Google Classroom are widely used, and uptake has rapidly accelerated in the last few years with widespread adoption of inexpensive Google Chromebooks. Like higher education, most K–12 platform deployments are examples of integrating technology into the old system rather than transforming the core learning process. They facilitate textbook replacement and open content utilization. Stronger deployments support some level of personalization and extend learning opportunities by allowing learners to learn at anytime, in any place.

Platforms have been relatively quick to transform commerce and the consumer space. Why have platforms been slow to make an impact in education?

Delivering a public service like education is very different than business to business (B2B) or business to consumer (B2C) markets. In efficient B2B or B2C markets, businesses can quickly deploy products, feedback is rapid and direct, scale is rewarded, and capital flows to promising investments. Access to cheap devices and ubiquitous broadband rewards early and effective platforms in a winner-take-most climate (such as services like Uber, operating systems like iOS, and retailers like Amazon).

Public services are framed by policy and paid for with a mixture of local, state, and federal investment. That should (but doesn't always) promote equitable service delivery, but it always comes with a lot of strings attached. In the last 20 years, many federal programs were layered on top of the idiosyncratic

LEARNING PLATFORM PROBLEMS

Most learning platforms lag behind consumer platforms in functionality by about five years for many reasons, including complicated adoption and procurement processes, less product investment and innovation, compliance requirements, and the need to match features to a particular form and level of education. Three top challenges include:

No portability. Platform updates in formal and professional learning exhibit an increased focus on learner experience, personalized learning, and alternative signaling (e.g., an emphasis on building portfolios and acquiring micro-credentials). However, few platforms offer a portable, Facebook-like place that allows users to freely customize and share their experience.

Not intelligent. With widespread use of analytics and artificial intelligence in consumer platforms, there is surprisingly little use of adaptive technology, data analytics, and smart nudges to improve learning behaviors. These are increasingly added to learning environments through specific tools (e.g., DreamBox in elementary math, and Civitas data tools in higher education) rather than embedded in platforms.

Not interoperable. While content management systems may enable more mix and match learning, much of assessment management remains a proprietary maze of walled gardens. Modern learners get more feedback from assessments built into digital experiences, but it remains difficult to combine multiple sources into a mastery tracking and reporting system.

American history of local control of education, resulting in patchwork of regulation that behaves very different than an efficient consumer market.

But it's not just the bureaucracy that some blame. There are two critical factors that make education different from the consumer internet. First, it is compulsory. Required attendance by students and required platform use by teachers can dampen the perceived need for high engagement experiences and environments. Teachers and students often put up with weak tools compared to tools they choose for personal use.

For driven professionals, goal-directed behavior may take the place of compulsory requirements allowing them to slog through flat sequential online courses. But self-activated, self-directed learners are few and far between; for most people, learning is relational and happens in community. Which brings us to the second difference: education is a complex, long term, multi-dimensional undertaking. By its nature, it is an intermediated enterprise.

New products create new opportunities, but this requires schools, districts and networks to adopt new tools, design and deploy new learning experiences. Transformation requires reconceptualized learning experiences matched with platform capabilities. Many of the networks we have discussed are attempting to innovate learning experiences and platforms while simultaneously seeking to bring the promise of personalized learning to scale. They combine shared goals and culture, powerful tools, and professional learning opportunities.

Schools like the Samueli Academy, in Santa Ana, California, directly illustrate the power of networks. A group of community leaders picked a proven school model, hired a talented staff, and now deliver vital services to young people who need it most. The Echo learning platform, used across the New Tech

AltSCHOOL

San Francisco startup AltSchool operates four small elementary schools in the Bay Area and New York. Rather than rolling out hundreds of branded storefront schools, the AltSchool team is licensing the platform to new and existing "partner" schools.

Founded by Max Ventilla, former Head of Personalization at Google, the AltSchool learner experience is a modern Montessori model—a personalized learning environment focusing on whole child development where students move on when they are ready, and learning is contextualized and expands beyond the classroom walls. The mixed-age learning environments range from 35 to 100 students.

Max started by hiring great teachers and trying to backmap from their work. They put engineers in the classrooms to codify practices and found a lot of variance that made it difficult to deliver on the promise of adding efficiency to an educator's workflow. They built a foundational curriculum based on a learning cycle that encourages learners to take initiative in their learning through engagement with real-world investigations.

The platform doesn't require a single learning model but is most valuable to schools and committed to cultivating learner agency through whole-child, personalized learning. The AltSchool team is trying to keep the solution simple and intuitive enough that it doesn't require a lot of training. The 2018–2019 school partner pipeline currently includes private schools and potentially a few progressive charter schools, with the goal of eventually supporting public school districts.

SAMUELI ACADEMY

Santa Ana is the dense urban center of Orange County, California. Ten years ago, local philanthropists Susan Samueli and Sandi Jackson rallied community concern about low graduation rates among low income and foster youth. They searched for school models that could maximize individual student attention; provide real-world, project based learning opportunities and exciting and fulfilling after-school programs; and support work-based learning and college and career readiness. They found the New Tech Network and became members. After applying for and receiving a charter, they opened a high school in 2013.

The Samueli Academy serves 480 mostly low-income students. The campus includes a residential village for 80 foster youth and their guardian families. They focus on engaging struggling learners and helping all of their students prepare for college. Students graduate at Samueli by presenting a four-year portfolio of work. Executive Director, Anthony Saba, thinks the New Tech Network "is on the right path and it is the answer for all kids. Not just underserved kids, but all kids in general."

Network, is another important part of the story. But unlike other sectors where platforms can quickly revolutionize service delivery, education is about relationships. Platforms can empower new learning experiences, but they happen in the context of sustained relationships, caring environments, and support services aimed at students and teachers.

Learning is different and more challenging than simple consumer applications. It takes skilled learning design, sustained relationships, and a transformative culture, as well as tools that support all three of these components. It also takes expertise to support learning with technology tools. School networks address these challenges by sharing learning models, platform tools, and teacher support.

LEARNER PROFILES WILL POWER PERSONALIZED LEARNING

With the following eight advances in learning science, technology, and standards, learning platforms will transform education and power personal learning journeys. Next-generation platforms will be easy to configure for specific learning and school models, gather data from many learning and context sources, and support a community of teachers and learners.

Feedback. Deciding what to learn, making a connection with the subject, and gathering feedback on your progress are all keys to learning anything. K–12 students in the US could use less standardized testing and more frequent and valuable feedback—from daily feedback on writing and problem solving to weekly reflections on collaboration, work habits, and project management skills. Automated and biometric feedback will help, but so will simple survey and feedback systems tracked over time. Frequent presentation and publication of work to external audiences further helps keep standards of quality real and dynamic.

Interoperability. Most US students benefit from multiple forms of instructional feedback every week, but little of it is delivered in a consistent fashion and easy to combine across classes, platforms, and technology systems. Technology vendors will need to allow schools to access their data and to share it with other vendors in common frameworks (the same way everyone in logistics agrees to use standard shipping containers).

In addition to agreements on standards, artificial intelligence will help spot correlation between various forms of assessment and feedback by analyzing big (anonymized) datasets of keystroke data. "Super gradebooks" will automatically combine many different kinds of formative feedback into a mastery tracker, which can in turn generate simple data visualizations. This important real-time information, and the recommendation engines they power, will help inform learners and help teachers co-construct and manage personalized learning journeys.

Scheduling. Far from isolating, these journeys will be highly social, just not with the same 30 students all day. Many learners will participate on project teams, benefit from tutoring in a skill group, connect with other learners around the world, and participate in arts, culture, work, and service-learning experiences in the community. Dynamic scheduling (and a network of self-driving vehicles) will help manage complex schedules. With locational awareness, platforms will spot real-time learning opportunities (e.g., you will receive a notification when you pass a museum which has an exhibit that would be helpful for your project).

Motivation. Young (and old) people are motivated by different experiences and are drawn to different interests. Learning and behavioral science will continue to unlock lessons of human performance—particularly motivational profiles that yield sequences of experiences that produce persistence and improve performance.

Portability. Personalized and competency-based learning, in K–12 and for life, will be unlocked by comprehensive learner profiles. These big, portable data sets are most likely to be made portable using Blockchain, a secure and distributed learning ledger (as described in Chapter Two). They will include a smaller official digital transcript (we call it a data backpack[4]) that will include more valuable information for teachers on day one at a new school. Additionally, parents and older learners will manage a comprehensive profile with downloaded data from digital learning experiences and a portfolio of learning artifacts that represent their personal bests. Learners and guardians will have the ability to share portions of the profile with tutors, after-school programs, summer schools, and online education providers.

User Interface (UI). Breakthroughs in UI—voice, gesture, and optics—could be transformative for some learners. After Elon Musk's new company Neuralink figures out how to make a direct connection between neurotechnology and computer interfaces, we'll be able to control computers with our minds.

Social and Emotional Learning (SEL) Supports. As most jobs become augmented by new technology, abilities like social awareness, empathy, and relationship management grow in importance. Productive ways to help young people develop self-management and social awareness will be a breakthrough. We see early forms of SEL already being integrated across the curriculum in a growing number of schools, and tools like biosensors, feedback systems, and smart nudges from digital assistants are likely to be part of smart SEL systems.

Assistive Technology. The advent of mobile and touch technology was a godsend for youth with special needs, particularly those on the autism spectrum. Advances in UI, translation, text-to-voice and voice-to-text services, and SEL supports will aid students that learn differently.

With advances in these eight categories, platforms will make it easier for teacher teams to create powerful learning sequences for and with young learners.

NOTES

1. https://marketbrief.edweek.org/marketplace-K–12/size_of_global_e-learning_market_44_trillion_analysis_says
2. https://www.svb.com/healthcare-investments-exits-report
3. http://mfeldstein.com/state-of-the-us-higher-education-lms-market-2015-edition
4. http://www.gettingsmart.com/publication/data-backpacks-portable-records-learner-profiles

PART TWO

TRANSFORMING SCHOOLS

POWERFUL
LEARNING

Personalized and Project Based

Isabella met us at the entrance to Katherine Smith Elementary School, a cluster of modular buildings behind a strip center in a low-income neighborhood in east San Jose, California. She escorted us to her fifth grade classroom where she shared a portfolio of work and proudly pointed to her persuasive essay—displayed as an example of quality work. The essay dealt with a classmate who had been diagnosed with a rare form of cancer. Isabella explained how her teacher had helped the class formulate a driving question about the nature of the cancer and potential for treatment. The question defined a set of project objectives including persuasive essays which were used to raise money for the sick classmate.

Katherine Smith Elementary is a neighborhood school in the Evergreen School District. In 2012, the low performing school was focused on low-level tasks and test preparation. When Principal Aaron Brengard took over, he recognized a need for a dramatic change in the learner experience and thought engaging project based learning (PBL) might be the solution. He brought a team to PBL World, a conference hosted by Buck Institute, to investigate if project based learning was the answer. When Brengard introduced the idea to the staff, he was very transparent about the changes that were about to take place, because he wanted to ensure that educators were both comfortable and excited about the shift that was about to happen.

After a visit to Napa New Technology High School with his superintendent in 2013, Brengard, with district support, wanted to implement the New Tech school model. A partnership with New Tech Network ensued and Katherine Smith Elementary became the first elementary school member of the New Tech Network. The journey from bite-size chunks of test prep to big questions, real work, and public products wasn't quick or easy. Yet combining the power of project based learning with a whole school model has played a key role in this school's transformation. After years of hard work and many iterations, Katherine Smith Elementary students own their own learning. They set goals, work on clear learning targets, produce high-quality products, present them to the school community, and collect them in a portfolio.

Despite the numerous challenges most students face, student agency, confidence, and ownership of learning is evident from the minute you step foot on Katherine Smith Elementary's campus. Not only do students serve as ambassadors and lead tours, but school leadership also has complete and genuine confidence in their ability to do so.

Principal Brengard saw a student ambassador program at a Napa New Tech High School and enthusiastically brought back the idea to his own staff to try. In addition to showcasing student work at Smith, Brengard wanted the student ambassador program to increase student agency and social belonging. Through the student ambassador program, students learn to plan and manage an agenda, and practice speaking, listening, and facilitating skills on tours. Each student sets personal goals as an ambassador. A student who was working hard to improve in her speech classes decided that giving tours to new people would be a good way for her to practice her public speaking skills. After each visit, Principal Brengard debriefs with the ambassadors and asks what they learned and what they will do better next time. Students have voice and choice, authentic tasks, and receive critique and feedback and reflect after the experience.

Katherine Smith Elementary is one of the best elementary examples of personalized and project based learning we have seen. The school, along with other district schools, joined the New Tech Network to continue its growth and learn together with other elementary schools adopting the national model.

NEW TECH NETWORK: THE ORIGIN STORY

Napa New Technology High School was created by the Napa School District when local businesspeople came together in 1996 to develop a high school where students would learn the skills necessary to succeed in the new economy. For founding teachers like Paul Curtis (who is now Director of Platform

Development for the New Tech Network), three things were different about Napa New Technology High School 20 years ago: it was small, with about 100 students per grade level; the integrated curriculum was project based; and there was a computer for every student.

On a tour, you first notice the double classrooms where traditionally separate subjects are combined. Teachers work together to design relevant projects that combine learning objectives from different subjects like math and science, and English and social studies. Students work in teams directing projects that may last for weeks and result in publications and presentations. Each project is assessed for communication, collaboration, knowledge, and critical thinking. They are also assessed for demonstrating personal agency (the capacity of the learner to act as an advocate for their own success, to complete work on time, do their best, and persist through difficulty—what Carol Dweck calls *growth mindset*).

After strong results from the first few graduating classes, a nonprofit organization was formed in 2001 to promote replication. With a $6 million grant from the Bill and Melinda Gates Foundation, the New Tech Network (NTN) set out to open 14 schools over three years. NTN founders had the insight to encourage the use of common tools alongside their project-based approach, making it the first platform network in education.

One of the first replication schools was Sacramento New Tech, where NTN Chief Operating Officer Tim Presiado was a founding teacher. Today, NTN supports about 200 schools, 90% of them in school districts (the remaining 10% are charter schools, most of which are formed by school districts).

NTN does not operate schools; communities partner with the network to provide school design, planning, training, and coaching.

"I had the privilege of being part of the opening of the third school in the Network," Presiado reflected. "As I step back now and look at what it means to have nearly 200 schools in our Network and of the value of being able to learn with and from teachers and leaders across the Network, I realize that I've been part of a movement . . . . What started as replication has become so much more, and I see clearly now that the real value of our partnership with schools and districts is around that network connection and the resources and learning we've co-developed together."

Schools in the New Tech Network share a project based learning model and a school design with double blocks that support integrated and applied learning—complex projects that ask big questions and require high quality public products. With a focus on deeper learning and school-wide learning outcomes, New Tech schools promote agency—students receive feedback (as well as communication and content knowledge) on every project.[1] Thanks to a diversity of school designs, the network illustrates the power of rigor, relevance, and relationship in neighborhood schools and schools of choice.

The New Tech learning model is supported by Echo, a learning platform with a library of projects that teachers can use or adapt with assessment rubrics and a standards-based gradebook that aligns to the deeper learning skills students will need in college and career. NTN was the first network to share a learning platform, an idea that most districts and networks now embrace.

NTN works with school districts in multiple ways to support school innovation and develop change management expertise.

CROSS COUNTY HIGH SCHOOL

In rural south Arkansas, Cross County High School (CCHS), a member of the New Tech Network, has been recognized for demonstrated success in closing the opportunity gap for underserved students.[2]

In the economically challenged, sparsely populated, 300-square-mile school district, farming is the main source of income in the area. People who do not farm drive long distances to work. "For most students, postsecondary education is now a necessity to reach the middle class, and the students we serve need someone to help them be successful in the postsecondary world," said retired Cross County School District Superintendent Carolyn Wilson.

In response to low postsecondary enrollment rates, Cross County High launched the College and Career Access Program (C[3]) during the 2014–2015 academic year. The program provides guidance and support to students and alumni to level the playing field. Support includes:

- Implementing curriculum, strategies, and guidance carefully designed to help students understand that postsecondary experiences are possible for them;
- Planning trips to show students what is possible— including a college trip for every student, grades 7–12;
- Providing students, parents, and community members with the resources and guidance necessary to help those around them achieve their goals;
- Designing and launching a college and career course for all eleventh-graders;
- Planning job shadowing experiences for all eleventh-graders;

- Providing ACT boot camps to students prior to the ACT; and
- Providing guidance and support to CCHS alumni throughout college.

Superintendent Wilson and her colleagues knew traditional internships were valuable but logistically and financially impractical in such a remote district. To address these issues, they created a virtual internship program to provide authentic work experiences. With over 40 mentors identified, Cross County High is offering internships that vary from marine biology to filmmaking, with mentors located around the world. New Tech Network coaches helped the Cross County team frame their challenge as projects, much like the projects they assign to students. The staff was surprised and pleased with the positive response to their requests to become virtual mentors.

On-site and virtual coaching, as well as national and regional convenings build teacher and principal capacity.

Network results have been consistently strong: 92% of students graduate, 70% enroll in college, and 82% persist in college. All the schools have become valued options in their community.[3]

After initially starting as a network of high schools, the New Tech Network now includes middle and elementary schools and is growing by about 25 new schools each year. In addition to helping districts implement the school model in new schools, and redesigning existing schools or academies located within comprehensive schools, the New Tech Network also provides system-level design and coaching to district partners to create change management structures that enable districts to spread the New Tech practices across districts.

PROJECT BASED LEARNING DEVELOPS LIFELONG SKILLS

Projects bring students into contact with new concepts and skills through a problem, context, or scenario that makes those new ideas worth knowing. Traditional, didactic methods of teaching ask students to learn because that is what their teacher is asking them to do. It makes sense to try to make sure learners are equipped to solve problems before they get to them, but unless students have a reason to learn something it is hard for new information to have any meaning. Learners often do not engage with new information until they try to do something with it. As a result, just-in-time personalized learning supports (including small group tutoring or assigned units that deliver targeted instructional resources based on student needs) during a specific challenge complement planned skill progressions prior to a project.

As Gregg Behr discovered in Pittsburgh, project based learning is more engaging than traditional teaching, and encourages young people to come to school, work hard, and persist in their learning efforts. It also is uniquely well-suited to developing a suite of future career skills like problem-solving, collaboration, critical thinking, and communication.

Project based learning engages students in their own success. Compared to a teacher-led unit of study, project based learning requires students to manage a multi-step project on their own or as a member of a team. Teachers at project-based elementary schools like Katherine Smith Elementary provide more structure, direction, and support for projects than at high schools like Napa New Tech, where students have more voice and choice in project design and more management responsibility.

Project based learning may be the most important career skill for young people headed for a project-based world. Four out of ten young people will enter the gig economy by stringing together a series of short-term assignments.[4] Perhaps as many will conduct their work for employers as a series of projects. Rather than a career in the traditional sense, the majority of young people will string together a series of projects—some as contractors, some as employees—into a working life with varying phases. Learning how to frame, staff, resource, and manage projects are critical career skills. Project based learning is an important way to apprentice students into being expert adult learners by involving them in the choices that need to be made about learning.

It is easy for teachers to get started with project based learning, but it is harder to do it well. It is challenging to set a high bar for high quality project deliverables and assess projects objectively, especially when they are all different. It is a challenge to support students with low level skills engage in challenging projects. It takes a strong learning culture along with careful monitoring and individual assignments to mitigate the "free rider" problem of loafing team members. There is a balancing act to providing enough (but not too much!) formative feedback and support. And finally, it takes thoughtful design to avoid big knowledge gaps resulting from a string of various projects. In order to do all of this well, teachers must learn to collaborate with their peers to design and improve projects.

A new generation of schools is blending the best of personalized learning and project based learning to address these challenges. They value deeper learning and development of success skills (growth mindset and social emotional learning) and track competency in all outcome areas. They use a variety of grouping and scheduling strategies to offer students a rich and varied learning experience. And they provide customized supports to build individualized skill fluency, which allows students with learning gaps to fully engage in challenging projects.

COMBINING PERSONALIZED AND PROJECT BASED LEARNING

The New Tech Network combines project-based and personalized learning—two approaches that may be philosophically aligned but pose significant operational challenges in the classroom. Teachers frequently face competing initiatives, insufficient planning time, inadequate resources, and ineffective professional development. Despite these challenges, and with the aid of a capable platform, the union of these two approaches has the potential to better engage and prepare students. Combining these two approaches within rural, urban, and suburban school settings with local talent and limited resources makes the New Tech Network's efforts worth emulating.

A growing number of charter school networks have developed unique combinations of personalized and project based learning. The most well-known is Summit Public Schools, a managed network of 11 West Coast schools that made its learning platform available to middle-grade teacher teams in over 330 teacher teams, supporting more than 54,000 students nationwide through a program called Summit Learning. Summit schools sequence four types of learning experiences aiming at outcomes in four categories:

- Personalized learning playlists to boost content knowledge;
- Projects to build cognitive skills;

- Mentorship and community time to develop habits of success; and

- Expeditions to apply knowledge and skills to real-life situations

Like Summit, Brooklyn LAB Charter Schools are among the best examples of a team simultaneously developing a next-generation learning environment and platform. Building on the Ed-Fi data standard with support from the Michael and Susan Dell Foundation, the Cortex platform is highly configurable. According to Brooklyn LAB Executive Director Eric Tucker, "LAB is increasingly engaging students in authentic, rigorous, relevant, and collaborative projects that are designed for complex learners and students with diverse ability levels. Whether the project is designing an academic program for high schools of the future, health centers for disaster relief, treatments for drug-resistant malaria, or a supply list for a wilderness survival trek, LAB increasingly uses projects to fuel learning." Given the diverse learners LAB serves, each project has multiple access points and distinct roles that enable a full range of students to engage and succeed supported by Cortex goal-setting, scheduling, and learning playlists.

Thrive Public Schools is a joy-filled K–12 San Diego network that combines personalized and project based learning. The urban schools in this network serve diverse students with individual skill-building and extended projects that culminate in public exhibitions. Thoughtful rubrics help teachers provide feedback on content knowledge and social emotional learning. Addressing a common concern about a "Swiss cheese problem" with project based learning, Thrive founder Dr. Nicole Assisi said there was no risk of learning gaps given their approach to personalized learning. While blended learning rotations fill in content gaps, "project based learning is necessary to engage learners, to build enthusiasm, and support authentic work and exhibition," said Assisi. "If school is just skills building and no application," she added. "where's the joy?"

Workshop School, a high school in Philadelphia that opened in 2013, seeks to unleash the creative and intellectual potential of young people to solve the world's toughest problems. Each day is divided into two flexible blocks of time, with the morning focused on project work and the afternoon focused on skill-building resources or in small seminars. Students progress through the school based on demonstrated mastery of applied knowledge and skills as well as project performance. Through this design, the school is attempting to demonstrate that deep, project-infused personalized learning can work for 100% of high-poverty, at-risk urban student populations in contrast to the "No Excuses" models.[5]

Da Vinci high schools are just south of the Los Angeles airport. On a spring 2017 visit, we witnessed students working collaboratively on a human rights presentation, designing a marketing campaign for a local company, creating displays for a community performance, analyzing the financial decisions of the European Union, and tending an urban garden. Students received individualized math and English support as well as comprehensive college planning and placement in an environment where every student is known and cared for. The four small, project-based high schools were adopted by the local elementary district to form a unified district, and share a beautiful new complex in El Segundo, California.

Like Thrive, Brooklyn LAB, Workshop, and Summit, Da Vinci is a Next Generation Learning Challenge grant winner. Da Vinci, Brooklyn LAB, and Summit won three of the ten $10 million grants from XQ: The Super School Project.

MOBILIZING SUPPORT FOR NEXT GENERATION LEARNING

Formed in 2010 with support from the Bill & Melinda Gates Foundation and the Hewlett Foundation, Next Generation Learning Challenges launched grant programs to support 10 new breakthrough postsecondary degree programs and 58 new breakthrough secondary schools. Support was also provided for dozens of blended learning, open-source courseware, learning analytics, and deeper learning tools.

In 2013, the Broad Foundation and the Michael & Susan Dell Foundation added their support to six regional funds. Partner organizations include CityBridge Foundation (Washington, D.C.); The Colorado Education Initiative; LEAP Innovations (Chicago, Illinois); New Schools for New Orleans; New England Secondary School Consortium (working in five New England states); and the Rogers Family Foundation (Oakland, California).

Next-generation models fuse aspects of blended, competency-based, personalized, and student-centered learning into a coherent whole. They are activated by project-based approaches and staked to rigorous, college and career-ready outcomes. Each school represents a unique model but all support the MyWays outcome framework, which consists of 20 competencies that cover content knowledge, creative know-how, habits of success, and wayfinding abilities.

Harmony Public Schools, a Texas network of 54 STEM-focused schools, used a federal Race to the Top grant to incorporate project based learning into their blended learning model. With frequent demonstrations of learning, the interdisciplinary model is called Students on Stage (STEM SOS). The online Harmony PBL Showcase is designed to promote and share exemplary student work that can serve as valuable learning and teaching tools for students, parents, teachers and other educators.

Design Tech High uses design principles to personalize the learning experience for high school students in Redwood City, California. "Competency-based learning means not giving up on a kid until they get it," said founder Ken Montgomery. Every week teachers mark students as ahead, on track, or off track using multiple forms of formative assessment. Students' schedules are flexible to ensure that each student gets the right support at the right time.

Beginning in 2007, Rocketship Public Schools pioneered an elementary blend of face-to-face and online learning in a Bay Area network. Inspired by the innovation, two South African MBA students visited Rocketship and launched SPARK Schools in Johannesburg in 2012. The flexible competency-based model allows students to move at different rates in reading and math. They also added design thinking projects to the Rocketship blend. On a visit in 2015, we saw fourth-graders present smart city dioramas made of recyclable materials.

Like these managed networks, thousands of school districts are combining the benefits of personalized and project based learning. Notable elementary examples include:

- Cesar Chavez Multicultural Center is a three building K-8 school serving 1,000 students from a low-income neighborhood on the south side of Chicago. Students benefit from thoughtful projects, blended learning, adaptive learning software, an extended day, and a data ninja principal.

- Horace Mann Elementary in Washington D.C. is the best example of an academic program, culture, and facility integrated around shared values of collaboration and connection, sustainability and stewardship, and choice and invention. The faculty values complementary approaches: one that offers students direct instruction, and one that offers a broad, constructivist approach that allows time to go deeper into areas of interest.

- EPIC Elementary in Liberty Missouri is an innovative, project based learning community designed to inspire students to be creative and think big. Serving 300 learners in the renovated district office, the EPIC architecture features double classrooms and partner teaching, iPad-powered blended learning stations, and extended projects. The pilot school is beginning to change structures and practices in the Kansas City suburban district and beyond.

- Design39Campus is a student-centered, design-focused, project-based K-8 school in Poway, just north of San Diego. Students work in large, open classrooms on their own, in project teams, or in big groups.

Eight notable high schools include:

- With support from Carnegie Corporation, Denver Public Schools incubated the Denver School of Innovation and Sustainable Development, where design thinking is central to achieving in four outcome areas: personal academic excellence, lifelong learning and citizenship, innovative thinking and action, and transformative leadership. Personalized learning is powered by the Summit Learning platform. Projects are aligned with the Buck Institute, and students frequently learn in the community.

- e3 Civic High is located in San Diego's spectacular new downtown library. Students learn through a mixture of self-paced online instruction, teacher or student-led small group instruction, direct instruction, and problem-based and project-based work. They also benefit from strong supports and extended learning opportunities.

- Casco Bay High School is a small, project-based public high school in Portland, Maine. Founded in 2005, Casco Bay serves as a mentor school in the EL Education network. Casco juniors engage in a long-term interdisciplinary project to demonstrate learning.

- Boston Day and Evening Academy has proficiency-based pathways that allow students to progress based on demonstrated mastery rather than seat time. Students benefit from wraparound services, digital tools that help create a personalized approach, and a school that is open 12 hours a day. In this format, self-paced, alternative education meets adventure-based leadership training and blended learning.

- Science Leadership Academy is an inquiry-driven, STEM-focused, and project-based school in Philadelphia. Every classroom provides evidence of their shared values of inquiry, research, collaboration, presentation, and reflection.

- Quest Early College High School north of Houston has a great student-led service learning program. About 90% of graduates (many of whom are first-generation college students) leave with an associate's degree.

- Phoenix Coding Academy focuses on computer science and multiple technology pathways through inquiry and project based learning. Students address big problems and learn how to use computation as part of the solution.

- Vista High is a large comprehensive school north of San Diego. After initial success with personalized learning, the school applied for and won a $10 million XQ grant to add project based learning focused on exploring, analyzing, and developing ethical solutions to global problems addressed by the UN Sustainable Development Goals. The student-centered culture is aimed at embracing diversity, fostering inclusion, and teaching students that the personal is global and the global is personal.

Many of these next-generation models reference the Buck Institute Gold Standard for project based learning. In unique ways, they incorporate Buck's Essential Project Design Elements: a challenging problem, sustained inquiry, authenticity, student voice and choice, reflection, critique and revision, and public product.

Project based learning features extended challenges that promote student engagement and, when well-conceived and supported, develop critical thinking, creativity, collaboration, and strong oral and written communication skills. Projects teach students to work independently, set timelines, and persist

XQ: THE SUPER SCHOOL PROJECT

As challenges and opportunities in our world change faster than ever, too often our schools aren't changing fast enough to help students meet those challenges. With that premise and $100 million from Laurene Powell Jobs, the XQ initiative set out to help America rethink high school. XQ issued a request for proposals and invited teams to engage in a discover-design-develop process supported by well-developed knowledge modules. After several phases that processed over 700 applications, 10 Super School grantees were announced in 2016.

through difficulty—all key to college and career success. Projects can tap students' altruistic interests by focusing on a community need.

The aim of personalized learning is to tailor the learning experience to the specific needs of individual students by holding the individual growth of students as the primary design driver for teaching and learning. Personalized learning usually aims at accelerated skill development to enable them to engage in grade level challenges—the reading, writing, and problem solving abilities to take on complex projects.

Districts and networks that are attempting to marry project-based and personalized learning attempt to balance student interest with important learning objectives, empower teachers and students as designers of learning, and encourage quality student products. With preparation and real-time support, project based learning can be used successfully with all students.

Benefits of personalized learning	Benefits of project based learning
• Gap identification and rapid skill acceleration • Detailed tracking and reporting of individual student progress and performance against multiple learning objectives • Instruction and assessment of critical college and career skills • Accelerated skill development	• Empowers students as designers, and engages them in learning how they learn • Connects student passions and interests, and develops agency and creativity • Authentic tasks create meaning and context for learning, and promote critical thinking • Develops collaboration and project management skills

There are six ways that project based learning supports personalized learning:

- **Teacher's role:** Personalized and project based learning shift the teacher's role to "guide on the side."

- **Agency:** While blended and personalized learning may be directed by a teacher or adaptive learning algorithm, project based learning almost always incorporates student voice and choice.

- **Meaning:** Projects create a reason to learn important content. Project based learning is designed to address the reality that "it's not what you know, but what you can do with what you know."

- **Time:** When projects direct student learning and self-management, teachers can provide individual and small group instruction.

- **Collaboration:** Most projects involve students working together to solve a complex problem, and even individual projects are often layered with purposeful structures for students to collaborate, share learning, and provide each other feedback. When students regularly work with a wide variety of peers, it builds school culture and relationships, helps them see diverse perspectives, and encourages them to enjoy learning as a social enterprise.

- **Breadth:** PBL reveals a wider range of student strengths and weaknesses. By exposing students to a wide range of real and simulated projects and problem solving scenarios, we allow them to perform in more contexts.

NETWORK TOOLS FOR PERSONALIZED AND PROJECT BASED LEARNING

A combination of six new tools and strategies is (or soon will be) powering personalized project based learning:

Diagnostic and adaptive tools. One of the most important advancements in personalized learning in the last decade is the development and widespread K-8 adoption of adaptive math and reading software (including i-Ready, Dreambox, and Reasoning Mind). They quickly zero in on a student's reading and math level and spot the texts and problems at the right level, which helps point teachers to topics that the student is ready to work on next.

Leading adaptive tools also allow teachers to assign particular units—a useful strategy in preparation for an upcoming project or to address a real-time need during a project.

Project based learning tools. New platforms (including Cortex, Empower Learning, New Tech Echo, and the Summit Learning platform) help teachers adapt or develop projects, build assessment rubrics, and support the process with personalized learning.

Creating personal learning plans for 50 students in an integrated project-based course can be overwhelming, but by using a learning platform, students can build project plans and assign themselves tasks to address key project goals.

Mastery-tracking. It is slowly getting easier to combine formative and project-based assessments into competency tracking systems. Some mastery trackers are incorporated into learning platforms while others incorporate formative assessment (MasteryConnect, Edmodo Snapshot, and OpenEd from

ACT) or are standards-based gradebooks (Engrade, JumpRope, or PowerSchool).

There is a chance that mastery tracking may reassert a coverage perspective which can unintentionally promote superficial coverage over depth and application. This can be avoided by tracking a narrower set of "power standards" of the most important and school-wide adopted learning outcomes. This approach helps students track progress on communication and critical thinking skills.

Public product. Producing, publishing, and/or presenting a final product is a distinguishing part of project based learning (and part of the Buck Institute Gold Standard[6]). Collaborative authoring (whether in Google docs or Office 365) further facilitates team projects. Blogging is a great way to express a commitment to writing across the curriculum. Online journals and magazines give students valuable publication experience. The 10 publications of Palo Alto High journalism students are world-class examples of what is possible.

Diplomas and Transcripts. Today, nearly 4,800 schools participate in the International Baccalaureate (IB) Programme—a curriculum, exam, and diploma system.

By 2019, hundreds of schools will use a common transcript platform that captures and presents demonstrated competencies and artifacts of student work in consistent formats. The Mastery Transcript Consortium is a network of independent schools committed to replacing courses and credits with demonstrated competencies and student portfolios. The Mastery Transcript is organized around performance areas rather than discipline-based courses, and mastery standards and microcredits rather than grades.

Dynamic scheduling. Schools that feature personalized project based learning feature big blocks of flexible time. In schools that combine personalized and project based learning, every day includes a variety of learning experiences:

- Advisory (heterogeneous group)
- Personalized learning time (individual)
- Small group instruction (performance level group)
- Project time (heterogeneous project team)
- Literature circle (heterogeneous group)

Inside what looks like a traditional class on the master schedule you'll also find a combination of personalized learning and project based learning in many next-generation networks. The Denver School of Innovation and Sustainable Development uses a classroom rotation model where teachers alternate on a weekly basis between facilitating personal learning time and project based learning by using daily formative data to provide small group instruction tailored to student's Personal Learning Plans.

New Tech Network member schools like The Community School in Spokane, Washington, have a portion of the day set aside for individual student projects. Many New Tech schools are moving towards more adaptive approaches to time that are more responsive to the demands and opportunities of project based learning and the pursuit of student interests. Being part of a network focused on learning together can make a tremendous difference in making this possible.

SECRET SAUCE: STUDENT AGENCY

The standards movement focused on "what" and "how"—detailed lists of student learning objectives and comprehensive evaluations of teachers focused on how learning is delivered to the learner. The result was less focus on the "why." When the education system imposes a what and how map, it often results in a lockstep approach that locates ownership within the system. A lockstep approach does not recognize each learner as a unique individual and does not ask young people to exercise agency.

Is knowledge or knowing "how" to learn more important? Is it better to have a map or a compass? Joi Ito, MIT Media Lab, recommends the compass: "A map implies a detailed knowledge of the terrain, and the existence of an optimum route; the compass is a far more flexible tool and requires the user to employ creativity and autonomy in discovering his or her own path."[7]

Educators who appreciate the importance of developing a strong compass favor personalized learning in a student-centered environment. Randy Ziegenfuss, a Pennsylvania superintendent, argues that a lockstep approach robs "learners of opportunities to develop the agility so needed in a world—now and in the future—of exponential change."[8] A learner-centered approach embraces the compass over the map.

During the 2015–2016 school year, Ziegenfuss led a community conversation in the Allentown suburb about what graduates should know and be able to do. They developed a profile of a graduate which serves as a compass for all learning activities.[9] In order to promote learner agency, teachers recognize learners as active participants in their own learning, and engage them in the design of their experiences and the realization of their learning outcomes in ways appropriate for their developmental level. They seek to engage learners' personal choice and voice, develop entrepreneurial attitudes and skills, and promote character through formal and extracurricular experiences.

During the standards movement, schools in the New Tech Network never forgot that student ownership of learning was important. Along with knowledge and thinking, collaboration, and communication, agency is one of the most important student learning outcomes assessed in every project in a New Tech school.

Agency is managing your own learning. New Tech schools share rubrics that identify the ability to develop and reflect on growth mindset and demonstrate ownership over one's learning.[10] Extended challenges help students see effort and practice as key to growth and success. Giving students the space to try, fail, and rebound builds confidence. Instilling the principles of agency helps students find personal relevance in their work and motivates them to participate actively, build relationships, and understand how they impact themselves and their communities.

New Tech students receive feedback on their growth mindset: how they work through challenges, use practice to get better, and independently reflect on their actions and decision making. They also receive feedback on their learning strategies: how they participate and stay focused, gather information, manage stress, and work with other people in order to do the learning they need to do.

School culture and the authenticity of learning experiences are key to developing agency. Culture and relationships should make student feel like they matter in the school community.

Authenticity means purposeful work that matters to students. Students will have a lot more persistence and agency if the work is purposeful through high-quality, project based learning. Having a growth mindset affects how a student persists in overcoming learning challenges. Persistence and the ability to manage one's own learning is an outcome that will serve a student well for the rest of their life, in any capacity.

Elementary school students tackle and monitor learning with a lot of teacher support in terms of what questions to ask, where to look, and how to gather information. A middle or high school student has a greater ability to ask questions, find resources, and find answers on their own. There is a gradual release of responsibility, with teachers providing more support at the lower levels and handing the work to students at the upper levels. The New Tech agency rubrics reduce the demand on teachers by focusing on fewer learning strategies, with more expectation of teacher support at the lower levels. Kindergartners need a lot of teacher support to manage frustration, work with other students, and manage their learning process, so the focus is more on social and emotional learning—managing emotions and dealing with frustration.

The staff at Washington Discovery, in Plymouth, Indiana, wanted to address and develop a growth mindset with their third-grade students. By having the students prepare for a 5K race, the students were able to focus on growth mindset in a tangible and concrete way. The students read about agency in abstract ways and then trained for the race and encouraged others to join the race. In addition, they had a community partner and raised money for an accessible playground for differently-abled students. This allowed them to learn about the challenges that others may face, and how others persist in spite of those challenges. The driving question for the Discovery

Dare to Dream project was "How can we convince people to do something even if it is challenging?" Student tasks within the project included five-paragraph persuasive essays, T-shirts with handmade designs, commercials for the run, and a map of the path—all culminating in the fundraising race.

Given the novelty and complexity young people are likely to experience in the world, they will need a strong compass—or wayfinding ability, as described in the Next Generation Learning Challenges (NGLC) outcome framework called MyWays. They'll need grit—the ability to persist through difficulty—and a growth mindset—an appreciation that capability increases with effort. For all of these reasons, the 500 schools in networks that value deeper learning outcomes (including ConnectED, EL Education, the New Tech Network, and seven others)[11] foster a student-centered culture and use project based learning to build student agency.

With the growing national recognition that agency is vital for college and career success, thousands of districts and networks are reconsidering their lockstep systems with bite-size learning. They are adding projects and extended challenges to their curriculum, and more student voice and choice to their learning culture.

NOTES

1. See an example from i3 New Tech: http://www.newtechnetwork.org/news/project-i3-new-tech-academy-earns-national-recognition
2. https://newtechnetwork.org/resources/closing-opportunity-gap-cross-county-high-school
3. https://newtechnetwork.org/impact
4. https://blog.linkedin.com/2017/february/21/how-the-freelance-generation-is-redefining-professional-norms-linkedin
5. http://nextgenlearning.org/grantee/workshop-school

6. http://www.bie.org/blog/gold_standard_pbl_essential_project_design_elements
7. https://www.amazon.com/Whiplash-How-Survive-Faster-Future/dp/1455544590
8. http://workingattheedge.org/2017/05/27/compasses-over-maps
9. https://drive.google.com/file/d/0B7BE9WstMVbvVm84bWVDTXpsTUk/view
10. https://newtechnetwork.org/resources/new-tech-network-agency-rubrics
11. https://all4ed.org/reports-factsheets/deeper-learning-network-overview

DESIGN THINKING
The New Frame for School

"Design thinking is a human-centered approach to innovation that draws from the designer's toolkit to integrate the needs of people, the possibilities of technology, and the requirements for business success."
　　　　　　　　　　　—Tim Brown, president and CEO, IDEO

Jared was an unmotivated and struggling freshman at a traditional high school in Boise, Idaho when he learned about a new school where students use design thinking to tackle real challenges. Jared transferred to One Stone, where he became a budding coder and took responsibility for his own learning. "My favorite part of One Stone is the accountability you have for your own learning," said Jared. "When I'm working on a project, I have to work on that project myself—and if that project doesn't work out, I don't get a C; I continue working on that project until it works. There's not sitting back and giving up. You have to finish the project, because you have ownership of the project."

One Stone was born through Teresa and Joel Poppen's unwavering belief in the potential of youth, and the incredible outcomes that can emerge when students are armed with design skills and access to opportunities to deliver those skills. Their evidence suggests that young people can do more than we or they dreamed possible.

At the Foundry, a makerspace at One Stone, Jared learned how to make things using a laser cutter and a 3D printer. Jared built a computer network and learned to program in several languages. Everything at One Stone—the facility, technology, culture, design process, projects, and partnerships—is designed for learning. Students have voice and choice in their learning, and make up the majority of the One Stone board of directors.

With the help of teaching coaches, One Stone students apply the design thinking process to career planning and make a mind map of their strengths and interests to begin to identify their opportunities to make a contribution in the world. Inspired by Stanford's d.school and honed for eight years in three after-school programs focused on design, community service, and entrepreneurship, the design thinking process at One Stone is rooted in empathy, and guiding the development of the project with the end user in mind.

The process starts by trying to understand the problem by gathering data. That may include interviews, surveys, sensors, or developing data partnerships. Design thinking requires empathy, and always keeps the end user's perspective in mind.

By using data and empathy, the student defines the problem with an actionable problem statement, a "*how might*

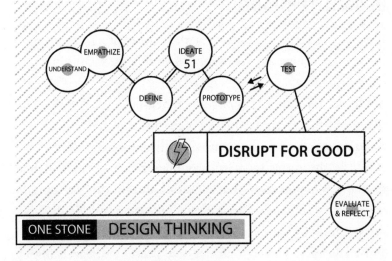

Figure 5.1   Design thinking at One Stone

we . . ." invitation to a solution. The iterative One Stone design process (see Figure 5.1) teaches students that it may take more than 50 attempts to solve a problem (hence the One Stone phrase, "51 it").

After sorting and selecting one or more ideas worth trying, it is time to pressure test with a prototype which can be any physical form: a storyboard, a physical model or a computer model. Then it is time to test prototypes with end users. Sometimes they love it, and sometimes not so much. Either way, designers gain valuable feedback, and then return to iterating before arriving at a final product.

With implementation, the One Stone team is seeking disruption for good, by "changing the way things currently are, to the way things *could be,* resulting in positive change that is also lasting."

The process ends (and often begins again) with evaluation and reflection. Outcome data is captured and evaluated. Reflections on lessons learned inform the next cycle.

DESIGN THINKING

If agency is the key mindset for the future, design thinking is the toolkit. There are two types of problems: technical problems with known solutions and adaptive problems that we have not faced. Life and leadership are increasingly filled with adaptive problems. Design thinking is flexible mindset and a structured approach to dealing with adaptive problems.

While the term has been around for five decades, design thinking was popularized at Stanford and by the founding of consultancy IDEO by David Kelly. Like the scientific method, design thinking can be applied to a broad set of opportunities and challenges. Through an iterative process, design thinking seeks solutions that are desirable, viable, and feasible. "Design thinking is a human-centered approach to problem-solving," said IDEO education lead Sandy Speicher. "It reflects how designers think and act—both mindset *and* tools," Speicher added. "It's solving problems to make the world better."[1]

Design thinking starts by imagining alternative futures. At One Stone, the problem-finding phases are called Understand and Empathize and include research, interviews, and field trips. The goal is to see the problem from the user's perspective. The next three phases—Ideate, Prototype and Test—are a period of iterative development where ideas are developed and tested in short sprints. Implementation and Evaluation are the final steps, before the process starts over.

Many school districts and managed school networks are good at execution and technical problem-solving. Most are not well equipped to cope with problems they haven't seen before. With the shift to digital learning, growing interest in personalization, and efforts to integrate project based learning, teachers, schools, districts, and networks find themselves designing all the time.

A growing number of districts and networks are adopting design thinking as central to their culture, teaching, and curriculum.

DESIGNING THINKING IN ENGINEERING EDUCATION

Olin College, a small innovative engineering school outside of Boston, is the best higher education example of project based learning infused with design thinking. President Rick Miller believes that an "urgent need is substantial improvement in the graduates' competencies in ethical behavior and trustworthiness, teamwork and consensus-building, effective communication and persuasion, entrepreneurial mindset, creativity and design thinking, empathy and social responsibility, interdisciplinary thinking, and global awareness and perception."

Students jump into projects on day one. Design Nature is a first-semester class where the first assignment in 2017 was to build things from cardboard that jump like animals. Students begin by building and applying a design thinking process. Interdisciplinary teams design a capstone project in the arts, humanities, social sciences, or entrepreneurship that involves a significant design problem with realistic constraints for an external partner. Most Olin projects result in a public product shared with the Olin community and often on a student portfolio website. Project teams gather three times during six-week projects for a 45-minute review session where they receive constructive feedback from peers and professors.[2]

Design thinking is also applied to curriculum development—sometimes on the fly. In 2016, a newly integrated 16-credit Quantitative Engineering Analysis sequence just wasn't working as designed. The professors and students paused, redesigned the course, and relaunched it—modeling the very sort of iterative development they are trying to teach.

If traditional schools answered the needs of the industrial revolution, Design Tech High School (or "d.Tech") in Redwood City, California is working on the solution for the technology revolution. They are using design thinking to personalize the learning experience for high school students to help them prepare for dramatic, fast, and unpredictable change.

"Students are caught between accelerating change and an old system; they're bored, overloaded, and stressed," said Ken Montgomery, the Executive Director and Founder of d.Tech. The d.Tech solution is extreme personalization and putting knowledge into action.

The design thinking mindset is central to d.Tech. As he points out, "it isn't about the next four years, it's about the next 40 years." Although they participate in regular design challenges, designing thinking at d.Tech is more of a mindset than a focused model. The process is infused in the culture and evident throughout the environment; and modeled in the work and interactions among students, teachers, and school leaders at every turn.

In a new, custom-built facility on the Oracle campus, Montgomery notes that d.Tech keeps the feel of the open campus concept from their humble origins in a warehouse. Students have access to the Oracle employee bus system and benefit from a close partnership with the tech company. Teachers use design thinking to update the d.Tech structure, schedule, and curriculum.

Teachers as design thinkers

Design39 Campus was the 39th school in the Poway Unified School District. Opened in 2015, design is central to the facility, culture, and pedagogy. In fact, principal Joe Erpelding say it is always in a state of redesign. He practices empathy by continually asking, "How can I value where everyone is coming from?" He acknowledges that we all walk with fear differently. He engages teachers and parents in an ongoing improvement dialog, asking, "In what ways will we be having a better conversation at this time next year?"

Teachers start the day at Design39 with design time, where they ask positive design-oriented questions of possibility, like "How might we?" Teachers use their design time to collaborate, share ideas, explore, and learn together; they share lessons and discuss what would constitute proof of learning. Erpelding uses his gift of time to rally the superpowers of his staff to unlock the genius of every student. Collaborative design thinking by teachers results in a vibrant learning environment where students use the same strategies to attack new problems, often asking "How might we?" in the process.

Design thinking begins with ethnographic research, often called *empathy research*, with a particular group of users. When teachers become "design thinkers," that means listening to students in deep ways. New Tech Network's Echo Curation Manager, Kelley McKaig said a big benefit from incorporating design thinking into personalized project based learning were the empathy interviews teachers conducted with students. "Going right to the source—students that you are planning for—was both impactful on our work and also opened our eyes to the complexity of personalization," she noted.[3]

Teachers using design thinking start with empathy, an exploration of the learner experience and the strategies and technologies that might improve learning. Conventional research methods, like focus groups and surveys, can be useful in pointing towards incremental improvements, but they may not lead to breakthroughs. Real innovation may take fresh thinking into new ways to achieve priority outcomes.

DESIGN THINKING LEADS TO COMMUNITY CONTRIBUTIONS

New Technology High School in the Napa Valley Unified School District in Napa, California has incorporated design thinking into project based learning. "We very quickly realized we couldn't approach design thinking as an add-on" said Principal Riley Johnson. Like almost all high schools, Napa New Tech relied on courses and credits to mark time and progress. When the school introduced design thinking, it encouraged the staff to begin thinking beyond the integrated courses common across the New Tech Network to the projects themselves. Rather than fitting projects into courses, the staff wondered if projects themselves could be the core architecture of the school. The staff decided to lead with projects rather than being trapped in a lockstep calendar and master schedule; that simple decision could change pacing (some students moving faster, some slower), how they supported students, and how they communicated student success (which was previously rooted in transcripts). This thought experiment led to a decision to launch the 2017–2018 school year with Design Thinking as a main focus.

The focus on design thinking has already changed Napa New Tech's approach to project based learning. "Focusing on empathy has allowed us to focus on the context in which we're working," said Riley. In school-wide challenges, students identify problems that they, their community, or society is facing. "All 400 students, through an empathy-building process, were able to find common interests and form cross-grade groups."

A group of freshman girls developed a solution for cell phone distraction to address smartphone temptation. Another group studied water usage in vineyards and recommended digital process improvements. And one group collaborated on a project about raising teen mental health awareness, in which they started with ethnographic interviews with people who struggled with these issues. They in turn used these interviews to create games to teach people about the effects of various mental illnesses. "The project was rooted in the human-centered aspect and led the authenticity," concluded Riley. Today, the games the project teams designed are used by two local health organizations with their clients.[4]

McKaig lled a design cohort of experienced New Tech teachers from elementary, middle, and high schools. The design group identified challenges in combining personalized and project based learning to tailor the learning environment to the specific needs of individual students. "Their willingness to innovate and learn together exemplifies the power of being in a network that values and supports active innovation," added McKaig.

Because they happily describe themselves as lifelong learners, these New Tech teachers wanted to learn how to be design thinkers. Most already thought about personalizing tasks within projects, inspired by what they learned from other teachers at New Tech conferences. The multi-outcome gradebook in Echo that tracks knowledge and thinking, communication, collaboration, and agency was a good start for research, but McKaig found that "the real insights occurred when conducting empathy interviews to determine the 'why' behind our actions and perspectives." Going directly to the source positively impacted project design efforts. Student interviews also allowed teachers to explore ways to further capitalize on student interests.

HOW DESIGN THINKING CHANGES PROJECT BASED LEARNING

"What if school was about discovering your gifts, what you love to do, and what the world needs? What if it was a place where you learned about how to make a meaningful contribution to others and the planet?" Kaleb Rashad is asking these questions at High Tech High in San Diego, California, which is well known for the ambitious integrated projects its students pursue. As the school director, Rashad is a visible cheerleader for human-centered design. "There is something that happens to a person when they are engaged in a real experience that has a benefit to someone else," Rashad said. "There is a sense of agency, voice, and personal standing in the world that is exciting and powerful and makes you question your mental models."[5]

As featured in the documentary *Most Likely to Succeed*, High Tech High encourages iteration leading to public exhibitions and publication. It is not just about the projects, Rashad explained, "but rather using projects as a window into humanity and as a vehicle for personal transformation."[6]

All good schools have a culture of revision, so what's new and different here? Traditional project management (and project based learning) is a sprint to a correct or predetermined outcome. Design thinking (or human-centered design) starts with problem-finding not problem-solving, and begins by asking questions about what people really need—a much more extensive and often more personal research phase than would be involved in traditional project based learning. Because design strategies are often used to attack adaptive problems without easy answers, solutions are prototyped in an iterative fashion. Teachers might ask learners, "How could you test your hypothesis quickly and cheaply?" If a project includes design thinking (understand, empathize, define, ideate, prototype, test) and implementation, it is a big, complicated undertaking. Be prepared to say, "I don't know."

If adding design thinking to project based learning is so complicated, why bother? Rashad points to a world that is only growing in volatility, uncertainty, complexity, and ambiguity. He argues that "we need Entrepreneurs, Producers, Innovators and Change Makers (EPIC), people who desire to make other people's lives better!" At High Tech High, they do that through powerful projects and deeper learning experiences.[7]

Much like the charter school High Tech High in San Diego, New Technology High School, in Napa, California, was opened in 1996 as a district-operated school with business community support and the goal of better preparing young people for a changing world. "As a school, we are big believers in the gig economy; the idea that the role of post high school life is becoming more project-based," said Riley Johnson, the principal of Napa's New Technology High School (also known as Napa New Tech).

"We believe that marrying PBL and design thinking provides a framework to ensure that no matter what students do after high school, they have the appropriate skill-set and processing ability," added Johnson. "By sharpening and putting more tools in their toolkit, we feel like we're setting up our students to have the opportunity to be successful no matter what they do."

By adding more iteration and prototyping to project based learning, the Napa New Tech team has seen success in earlier and more frequent presentation. Students present their first prototype at week four and received feedback from a public audience 20% into the scope of the project. This way, students are able to iterate several times. "By using the Design Thinking mindset, the revision and refining process is starting to become stronger," said Johnson.

Design thinking is also present in process improvement at Napa New Tech. The staff had noticed that, while valuable, student portfolios were becoming a checklist. "We had students who would wait until right before it was due and then try to get all the things on the list checked off and be done with it," said Johnson. Staff and students used design thinking to re-examine the portfolio process. After a nine month design process, "the result was a shift from a static webpage design to a comprehensive, four year blogging portfolio experience," said Johnson. Napa New Tech moved from "here is your rubric and what you need to finish" to finding authentic opportunities for students to reflect and share learning. "Our portfolio now lives with students throughout the four years and beyond," added Johnson. Napa New Tech students are using their portfolios to gain college admissions and internships.[8]

Adding design thinking to project based learning and supporting it with personalized learning strategies appears to be incredibly valuable, but is also very challenging—and why schools should work in networks to develop and deploy new learning models, tools, and professional learning opportunities.

NOTES

1. http://www.gettingsmart.com/2017/02/scheduled-design-thinking-as-pedagogy-for-students-and-educators
2. http://www.gettingsmart.com/2016/12/podcast-project-based-engineering-olin-college
3. https://newtechnetwork.org/resources/making-pbl-personal
4. https://newtechnetwork.org/resources/leader-spotlight-riley-johnson-new-tech-high-school-2-0/

5. http://www.gettingsmart.com/2017/02/getting-smart-podcast-10-leaders-on-high-quality-pbl-doing-it-well-at-scale
6. http://www.gettingsmart.com/2016/09/its-not-just-about-the-projects
7. https://www.hightechhigh.org/hth
8. https://newtechnetwork.org/resources/leader-spotlight-riley-johnson-new-tech-high-school-2-0/

CONNECTED TEACHING

Technology Enables Co-Creation

Pedagogy is a method of teaching. A newer term that includes more context variables is *learning model*. Learning technology has made it possible to conceptualize new learning experiences and sequences that combine face-to-face, hands-on and online learning activities. A learning model includes a set of desired outcomes, classroom practices and protocols; short and long-term tasks and learning experiences; a means of assessing outcomes; grouping strategies and rules that govern student progress; and norms for behaviors and collaboration.

Students at Roots Elementary, an innovative school sponsored and incubated by Denver Public Schools, rotate through different centers in a big, open room called the Grove. They check in to each center using their iPads and a QR code. Breakout rooms around the edges are for small group instruction. Founder Jon Hanover explains that about half the day is spent doing self-directed work—some with books and blocks, and some with game-based learning applications. Periodically, students are pulled from their self-directed work for small group instruction with a teacher. These students may vary by age, but they are all working on the same skill. Students spend about half the day in these groups, getting instruction targeted for their specific needs.

The rotational system at Roots is an example of a whole school learning model. A whole school model adds structure, staffing strategies, schedules, student and teacher supports, and information systems to a learning model to make it a complete system.

At Summit Public Schools, a network of some of the most innovative secondary schools in the world, the learning model starts with a thoughtful definition of outcomes which drives a combination of personalized learning, project based learning, mentorship, and work-based learning. With help from Chan Zuckerberg Initiative engineers, the Summit Learning platform queues four kinds of experiences related to the four outcome domains:

- Project time promotes cognitive skills.
- Personalized learning time promotes content knowledge.

- Expeditions support real-life experiences.

- Mentoring and community time promote habits of success.

The Summit School model includes 40 days of professional learning every year enabled by quarterly student expeditions which are taught by central office staff or partner organizations. When students participate in expeditions, teachers have time to visit other schools and work on their learning plan. Every week includes time to work with teammates and connect with "job-alikes" across the network.

Summit School is extending their platform network to teacher teams nationwide through their Summit Learning program. Over 330 teacher teams have received free access to the Summit school model, platform, and training. It is a bold new scaling strategy for Summit—and a new approach to philanthropy for the Chan Zuckerberg Initiative.

CO-CREATION ON PLATFORM NETWORKS

Platform networks share an approach to learning (a school model), common tools and systems (usually a learning platform), and an adult learning community where improvement thrives—a pedagogy, a platform, and a professional learning network (see Figure 6.1).

Most school networks launched after 2010, including Summit Public Schools, Alpha Public Schools, and Brooklyn LAB,

Figure 6.1 Three elements of platform networks

were built around a platform or a blended learning model. These managed networks share a school model, toolset, and support services. Like school districts, these networks also have governance and administrative responsibilities.

Some school districts, particularly smaller ones, operate like platform networks with a common approach to learning, a shared platform of information systems, and aligned support systems. North Carolina's Mooresville Graded School District pioneered a distributed leadership approach to their district-wide digital conversion.

Most large school districts utilize some version of a portfolio strategy (see Chapter Ten) where schools have the flexibility to develop or adopt school models or join networks. For example, the board of Denver Public Schools adopted a common graduate profile but supports the growth of networks including Beacon, DSST Public Schools, KIPP, Rocky Mountain Prep, and Strive.

For the first 20 years of the shift to digital, learning platforms like Blackboard delivered flat courseware to college students with little interaction other than an occasional quiz. By 2010, startup platforms like Edmodo incorporated a Facebook-like user experience making it easy to mix and match content, construct and assign unique tasks to groups, and facilitate text message-like communication threads. After the Apple iPad was introduced in April 2010, their application development platform got easier to use and, with the proliferation of smartphones and tablets, developers built applications for every conceivable use. Mobile traffic accelerated and it became clear that mobile use would become important in most sectors, including learning.

PERSONALIZED LEARNING REQUIRES AGREEMENTS AND BENEFITS FROM NETWORKS

"There are two things school networks need to get right early on: a shared vision for what excellence looks like in schools, and the supports needed to help educators realize that vision."

Alex Hernandez, who leads efforts to create new school networks for the Charter School Growth Fund, thinks charter school networks are one of the most important developments of the last two decades. "Charter schools are answering the question: what can great public school systems look like at scale? In the best charter networks, there is a lot of coherence. All the adults are rowing in the same direction and different parts of the school program reinforce each other."

In loose voluntary affiliations, Hernandez sees more variability and less value: "It's hard to get good at anything if educators can't agree on what is important. I don't see truly great schools where each teacher closes the door and figures it all out for their own kids."

At the top of his list of things good networks share is common expectations for what great teaching and learning looks like. Schools may use different approaches to the same end, so that students are intellectually challenged and deeply engaged. Classroom conversations are vibrant. There are clear strategies to help students who need more support.

"We love to say our schools will do project based learning and let students move at their own pace and teach

(continued)

social-emotional skills, but getting good at any one of those things takes a massive investment to do well," argues Hernandez.

Great networks make huge organizational investments to create these types of classroom experiences—it takes size to solve big problems in education. Hernandez says great networks often develop carefully-sequenced curricula, record videos of excellent instruction, curate thought-provoking readings, develop questions that encourage students to think deeply, create assessments that set a high bar for learning, and train teachers on specific classroom moves, among other supports.

While Hernandez sees the best networks getting tighter, it feels less oppressive than the scripted, managed instruction regimes of the last decade. The purpose-built networks in his portfolio are well-engineered systems. "In our best networks, expert teachers are distilling resources and practices that have produced great outcomes," says Hernandez, "and then these resources are refined as teachers across the network use them and provide feedback." Teaching roles are intellectually demanding but, like doctors in a health care system, the moral authority of best practices and proven success is recognized.

The shift to mobile is just one of the trends affecting the development of new learning platforms. A review of startups reveals six feature trends:

Cloud and mobile: Following consumer trends, learning platforms made the shift to the cloud and are slowly moving to mobile. For example: Instructure launched a mobile application for the Canvas LMS, fee-based cloud storage, and an app store to boost interoperability in 2013; they added a mobile app for parents in 2016.[1]

Mix and match: Learners, advisors, and algorithms can quickly combine resources from multiple providers into custom pathways. For example: Cortex from nonprofit InnovateEDU integrates learner profiles with the ability to build, customize, and deploy unit plans and playlists along a competency progression built for different grade bands.

Relationships and supports: Many formal and professional learning providers are paying more attention to learner relationships and support systems. For example: Motivis, an LMS developed by and spun out of Southern New Hampshire University, is a social learning community that supports student engagement and relationship building.

Competency: Developing, tracking, and supporting demonstration of competencies allows learners to move at their own pace. For example: Empower Learning is a competency-based LMS with standards-based progress reporting and transcript management.

Broader aims: Mindset, self-regulation, social awareness, collaboration are increasingly incorporated and tracked by platforms. Wellness and fitness are next. For example: Minecraft: Education Edition promotes social emotional learning.[2] Platforms like New Tech Echo track growth in collaboration and agency with each project.

Prediction: Machine intelligence will be built into all platforms in the form of predictions, recommendations, and smart nudges. For example: the Learning Navigator from nonprofit Gooru is a free, online tool that offers personalized pathways to help students reach their learning goals—a virtual GPS for learning.

Chief Executive Officer of the Hastings Fund, Neerav Kingsland, has a hunch that "in the future most schools and districts will be on educational platforms that combine human curation of content and algorithms to develop an instructional program from afar."[3] He predicts that "school operators will outsource many of the traditional roles of a Chief Academic Officer (CAO) to a platform," and, on average, the platform will be better. More specifically, school operators will outsource the CAO role to a network, one that shares a learning model, platform, and professional learning opportunities.

A few intrepid networks—including Summit Public Schools, Brooklyn LAB, and New Tech Network in partnership with Agilix—have developed their own learning platforms, giving them the infrastructure to support new innovations. These platforms are difficult and expensive to build right now. It's easy to invest over $100 million in a quality learning platform and that is likely to limit innovation until a few next-generation platforms become well established. In short, until it is easy for teacher teams to personalize learning and support student progress on demonstrated mastery, school model innovation and network growth will be dampened by platform shortcomings.

CO-CREATION ON THE NEW TECH PLATFORM

To meet the professional growth needs of educators and school leaders, the New Tech Network created Professional Learning @ NTN (PL@NTN), a series of in-person and online experiences and resources with a badging system that helps educators demonstrate and document their development.

Project design: The most common form of co-creation across the New Tech Network is project design. Teacher teams can review the project library on Echo and adopt and/or adapt them to meet the needs of their students, while aligning to specific state standards. Project design resources and learning outcome rubrics help teams develop new and exciting integrated projects.

Workshops: Chris Covey, District Instructional Coach for Van Wert City Schools in Ohio, appreciated the elementary workshop on how to incorporate literacy into projects. "That workshop was an 'aha' moment for our teachers who were struggling with literacy and how it fit into their projects. It was nice to get confirmation that they could teach literacy alongside projects and incorporate it into projects."

Online learning: Covey recalls an online workshop on problem-based learning, with one or two day performance tasks rather than three or four-week projects. The math-specific approach was not part of the original New Tech new school training, but Chris and his path teachers found the online course, additional resources, and idea starters all very beneficial.

Teacher connections: In addition to building individual capacities, PL@NTN is an opportunity for teachers to leverage the network expertise of NTN teachers and coaching staff. "PL@NTN allows me to connect with NTN teachers at other schools and with New Tech coaches," said Sara Costello, Instructional Coach for West Des Moines Community Schools. "It is nice to get to know other New Tech coaches with different specialty areas. It allows me to connect my school's facilitators with relevant experts."

Schools facing similar challenges or working on similar projects can connect and collaborate. "PL@NTN certainly offers the opportunity for network building and making connections with other NTN schools, added Costello."

Covey added that the connections were making Van Wert schools "more of a learning organization versus closing our doors and doing our own thing."

Badging: PL@NTN affords teachers the opportunity to earn microcredentials in 23 skill areas specific to the New Tech project based learning model. This badging program makes a complex set of interconnected practices more approachable. New Tech Network staff review badge submissions to ensure mastery of key skills and continued growth as PBL practitioners. Teachers who meet all criteria are recognized with specific microcredential badges and, when appropriate, umbrella badges as well.

While the badging program is designed to allow an individual New Tech teacher to improve core PBL competencies, several network schools use the program to structure their own professional learning program. Greenville Early College a high school in Greenville County Schools, Greenville, South Carolina uses the badging system in a small group format. Teachers independently work on the badges and come together to discuss each unit. This has allowed the school to build success through small team units.

Exemplars: The PL@NTN badging program provides exemplars of specific aspects of faciliatating project based learning. If a teacher is struggling in a specific area, he or she can look at an exemplar to see what another teacher across the network has done in a classroom. The badging course offers instructional coaches a curated resource library on the Echo platform.

Summer internships: Samueli Academy students do a 45-hour minimum summer internship between junior and senior year. It was a big challenge finding internships for all of the school's juniors and seniors. "We received great feedback after our first year. Both the businesses and the students had an overwhelmingly positive experience," said executive director Anthony Saba. Some students realized their internship was a field they were not passionate about—another valuable outcome. The carefully structured and sequenced work-based learning activities, which are co-created with business partners, prepare students to make informed college and career choices, allowing them to acquire the necessary college-and career-readiness skills.

"Value-creation is never the result of individual action," said author Niels Pflaeging. Rather, "it is a team-based process of working interactively, with-one-another-for-each-other." That describes team teaching in a network—a process of learning and creating together.

CITY AS CLASSROOM

One of the most exciting forms of co-creation emerging is place-based education, an approach to learning that takes advantage of geography to create authentic, meaningful, and engaging personalized learning for students.[4] Immersive experiences situate students in local culture, landscapes, and workplaces. Place-based experiences that are highly relevant and engaging contribute to deeper, richer learning. These experiences can boost student motivation, persistence, and appreciation for local communities.

While field trips qualify as place-based learning, the goal of place-based education is often to move up Bloom's taxonomy to analyzing, evaluating, and creating, and to move from simple applications to complex authentic settings—what NGLC calls situated learning.[5] This learning rooted in community often takes the form of projects, community-centered design challenges, or service learning initiatives. It offers relevance to students and teachers, infinite pathways to personalization, and tools for students to experience agency and a sense of ownership for community sustainability and improvement.

Place-based education design principles from Teton Science Schools can inform the development of location-based learning in any setting:

- **Local to global context:** Local learning serves as a model for understanding global challenges and connections.

- **Learner-centered:** Learning is personally relevant to students and enables student agency.

- **Inquiry-based:** Learning is grounded in observing, asking relevant questions, making predictions, and collecting data to understand the economic, ecological, and sociopolitical world.

- **Design thinking:** A structured approach to iterative solution development provides a systematic approach for students to make a meaningful impact in communities.

- **Community as classroom:** Communities serve as learning ecosystems for schools where local and regional experts, experiences, and places are part of the expanded definition of a classroom.

- **Interdisciplinary approach:** The curriculum matches the real world where the traditional subject area context, skills, and dispositions are taught through an integrated, interdisciplinary, and frequently project-based approach where all learners are accountable and challenged.

Field Education programs offered by Teton Science Schools engage students in watershed science, water quality testing, and field research. Both curricula enable personalized, student-centered learning projects around student interests.

Larry Rosenstock, founder of High Tech High, thinks of the city of San Diego as the text for learning. A carpenter and lawyer, Rosenstock sees "place as palette" and encourages teachers to co-construct place-based projects like integrated art and biology projects that benefit a local blood-bank, published watershed research, and a field guide to local birds and plants produced by elementary students.

Students at Casco Bay High in Portland, Maine engage in learning expeditions—extended integrated in-depth studies that explore questions of social justice. Expeditions involve field work and culminate in an authentic project, product, or performance. Past topics have included Portland's Working Waterfront, Flu Pandemics, and the BP Oil Spill.

Undergraduate students attending Minerva, an innovative new higher education model, live and learn in seven cities and participate in location-based learning experiences including research projects and internships. Students meet with civic leaders and do project work for top organizations. These place-based activities aim at building transferable capabilities that can be applied in unfamiliar situations.

Well-constructed place-based experiences like these four examples promote student agency by providing voice and choice in determining what, how, when, and where they learn. In regard to place-based education, Next Generation Learning Challenges (NGLC) notes that brain science has confirmed that students learn content more durably and transferably through authentic learning activities and that habits of success can be developed only in complex, socially situated experiences that require or enable learner agency.[6]

In order to have the time and resources to co-construct place-based learning experiences with students, teacher teams need the support of school leaders. Chapter Seven explores the development of collective capacity in learning organizations.

NOTES

1. https://www.canvaslms.com/news/pr/canvas-announces-new-first-of-its-kind-mobile-app-for-parents&122616
2. http://www.gettingsmart.com/2017/06/minecraft-social-emotional-learning-K–12-education
3. https://relinquishment.org/2016/12/23/future-rivalries-the-platform-vs-the-chief-academic-officer
4. http://www.gettingsmart.com/wp-content/uploads/2017/02/What-is-Place-Based-Education-and-Why-Does-it-Matter.pdf
5. https://s3.amazonaws.com/nglc/resource-files/MyWays_11Learning.pdf
6. http://www.gettingsmart.com/wp-content/uploads/2017/02/What-is-Place-Based-Education-and-Why-Does-it-Matter.pdf

LEARNING ORGANIZATIONS
Building Collective Capacity

To kickstart organizational learning, Chip Kimball, the new superintendent of the Singapore American School (SAS) asked his board for an appropriation of half of a percent of the budget for organizational learning, research, and development. The fund enabled 100 staff members to visit 100 schools in eight countries. Visiting the best schools in the world, presenting their observations to colleagues, and plugging into professional learning communities proved transformational for the 4,000 nursery to high school students.

The SAS strategic plan centered around a shift from content-focused, teacher-led instruction to skills-based, student-centered learning. Students help to shape high-impact learning experiences that deepen their learning and shift the focus from the teacher to themselves. This helps students develop the ability to demonstrate cultural competence and strong character while utilizing content knowledge to be critical and creative thinkers, as well as effective collaborators and communicators.[1] Creating a learning organization, particularly high-functioning professional learning communities, has been at the heart of the transformation.

Professional learning communities (PLCs), popularized by author Rick DuFour, were central to the SAS transformation. PLCs focus on collective learning for teachers through cycles of inquiry. Teachers collaborate in PLCs to set learning targets, refine academic offerings, and develop common assessments. PLCs answer the following questions:

- What is it that we want students to know and do?
- How will we know when they know and can do it?
- What do we do when students don't get it?
- What do we do if students have already gotten it?

PLCs drive curriculum consistency and encourage teacher teams to take collective responsibility for all students' learning, and ensure that faculty work collaboratively to leverage their expertise and analyze evidence of learning to improve their own practice and maximize each child's learning and growth.

There are several large online teacher networks including Teacher2Teacher, a Gates Foundation sponsored teacher social network with some job-alike communities that share tips and tools. Practice campaigns (e.g., encouraging one small classroom improvement) and cause campaigns (e.g., Teachers for Equity) are supported by blogs and social media exchanges.

More than 150 schools sponsored by national and regional funds of the Next Generation Learning Challenges (NGLC) are another example of a professional learning community. While NGLC grants are important, the faculty of these next-generation schools report that the community is even more valuable. NGLC provides tools and resources, convenings, and social media meetups. Educators on next-generation campuses open their schools to visitors, share their curriculum and tools as open resources, and actively contribute to multiple networks.

TEACHING TOGETHER, LEARNING TOGETHER

Approaching a traffic light, Kevin Gant, then a teacher at Nex+ Gen Academy in Albuquerque, a New Tech Network school, came up with a project idea about stopping distances—combining a bit of physics, a bunch of math, and some sociology. He wasn't teaching physics or math, so he blogged about the Stoplight Project and shared his thinking. Taking the invitation, Heather Buskirk, a Physics teacher in New York ran with the idea and blogged about it. Pleased with her students' experiences and learning, Buskirk used the stoplight project for her national board certification application. Project ideas, lessons, and resources whip around the New Tech Network like this every day.

A powerful practice observed in most secondary-level New Tech classrooms is the collaboration of two teachers working together to co-facilitate a course. By integrating subjects together, the course better reflects the way content and projects work in the world, with many subjects commingled. Since most secondary teachers are typically specialists in one subject area, New Tech high schools pair teachers together to collaboratively design integrated, cross-discipline projects. From there, that collaboration often extends into the actual facilitation of the projects. Most schools merge these integrated classes into a single course. For example, English 10 is often combined with world history to create a World Studies class, collaboratively taught by an English teacher and a social studies teacher. When this is done well, it is taught as one seamless class, as opposed to alternating between half of the time spent on English and half of the time spent on social studies. These courses are often double-blocked, so with two teachers, you have twice the class size as a single teacher. That is why most classrooms in purpose-built or renovated New Tech schools are double-size.

Team-taught integrated courses are among the most important elements of the New Tech high school model. Integrated courses create benefits for instructional design, instructional practice, and school-wide culture-building. Combinations that work well include English and Social Studies or Biology; Physics and Algebra II; and Biology, Health, and Physical Education.

BENEFITS OF TEAM-TAUGHT INTEGRATED COURSES

Project design: Allows more authentic project design since the work of the world is rarely siloed in a single discipline.

Iteration: When a teacher has a collaborating colleague to check in with about how things are working, and *while they are observing it*, projects and project execution tend to get better immediately.

Grouping: Teachers have more flexibility in grouping because there is a larger sample of students to draw from with a double-sized group of students.

Differentiation: When one teacher is running a skill-building workshop for students that have a specific need, the other teacher can supervise and support the students who aren't attending.

Modeling Collaboration: If you're asking students to collaborate with each other, team teaching gives them a model for what good collaboration looks like.

Behavior: Teachers will often tell you that there is a marked difference in student behavior when there is one teacher in the room versus two teachers in the room, and the latter is almost always preferable. When a student is having a bad day, team teaching allows one teacher to have a conversation with that student about their issues, while the other teacher ensures that the rest of the class is moving forward.

Student culture: Larger classes create another avenue for building student culture, because students see many other students in the class, creating a gestalt sense of the student body.

Adult culture: The presence of the course creates automatic practice at building adult culture in your building. Two people per grade level learn how to collaborate in their course, and that tends to spill over into full-faculty meetings. It also creates pressure to improve practice.

Sustainability: As a teacher, if you have a good partnership, it makes the work more sustainable. Having the built-in collaborator makes things so much easier.

Values: Integrated courses and the projects students produce provide a public platform to demonstrate school values. It shows that the school believes in integration and collaboration—and it is not willing to let it happen by accident.

LEARNING ORGANIZATION FRAMEWORK

As discussed in Chapter Four, New Tech Network is one of the largest and best examples of a platform network and growing by about 10% annually through school district partnerships that result in scaling new and redesigned schools across a district. Network schools appreciate the library of integrated projects, the tools for creating and assessing projects, and the virtual and onsite coaching.

The NTN team focuses on creating value for schools to join and to stay part of the network. Four keys to success include:

- The pillars of the New Tech model: Teaching that engages, outcomes that matter, culture that empowers, and technology that enables;

- Effective professional development and coaching that is differentiated for classroom teachers, administrators, and district staff;

- District relationship building: significant time supporting district leadership teams on school design and ensuring the conditions that support and sustain school transformation; and

- A commitment to continuous improvement and innovation that resonates deeply with schools and districts.

In order to help schools shift their focus from the initial work of implementing a new school model to the work of improvement, the New Tech Network developed the Learning Organization Framework (Figure 7.1). The framework is designed to guide the development and execution of short-term cycles of inquiry and improvement at the school level.

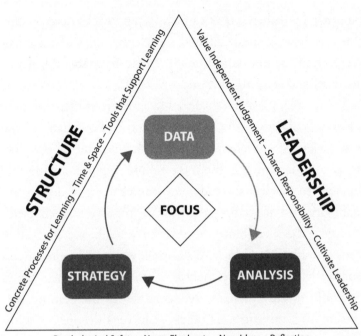

Figure 7.1 The NTN Learning Organization Framework

The framework also helps build the capacity of schools to learn and improve collectively—all in an effort to support schools as they get better at getting better.

NEW TECH NETWORK LEARNING FRAMEWORK

The interior portion of the framework represents a structured cycle of inquiry and process for improvement in relation to a specific focus. The central focus is the specific thing about student learning that a school wants to improve. The cyclical process around the focus names the major steps in any cycle of inquiry (and there are countless inquiry cycles across many fields that have been articulated). The three sides of the triangle represent the key conditions that tend to enable or impede organizational learning and improvement.

For example, if a school wanted to improve student writing, they could collect writing samples (Data) and conduct a structured review of student work (Analysis). As the school does this, two things emerge. First, the school might conclude that they need to coach their students around the use of descriptive vocabulary and academic language to improve written products across the curriculum. Second, they might recognize that 45-minute planning blocks do not allow enough time to collaboratively engage in the analysis of student work. As a result, they could modify their master schedule for the coming year to create a 90-minute time block each week devoted to adult learning and collaboration.

This example improvement process helped the school improve in two ways. First, they improved the quality of student writing by working through the structured cycle of inquiry. Second, they increased the capacity of the system to improve in the future by making a structural change—they got better at getting better.

The Learning Organization Framework is a key tool in the network's school leadership development efforts. NTN promotes a vision of school leaders as architects organizing the school's structure and culture to support adult and student learning. Case studies that document the use of the Learning Organization Framework are used as teaching tools at the network's national Leadership Summits.

Most professional development providers reinforce individual capacity building, however, the New Tech Network focuses on collective capacity building—helping schools learn how to learn together, collaborate effectively, and become highly adaptive systems. There are ample opportunities for individual educator professional development, through PL@NTN and through the Echo badging program. Learning together is critical for new models that value personalized learning and integrated projects. General training is less relevant to schools that adopt or develop unique models.

By matching design, technology, and professional learning, networks can provide a shortcut to coherence and performance. Networks providing relevant services at a fair price continue to grow and extend impact as a result.

NETWORKED IMPROVEMENT COMMUNITIES

"At the core of improvement research are the rapid iterative cycles of testing possible change ideas against data, revising, retesting, and refining," said Anthony Bryk, President of the Carnegie Foundation for the Advancement of Teaching.[2] Bryk urges organizing into networked improvement communities (NIC), a continuous improvement framework that can be used within one institution or across a network of like-minded organizations. "While our individual capacities may be modest, working together we can achieve much more," added Bryk.

There are two ideas at work here, and the first is making improvement science core to the work of schools. Bryk advocates for six core principles of improvement:

- Make the work problem-specific and user-centered.

- Variation in performance is the core problem to address.

- See the system that produces the current outcomes.

- We cannot improve at scale what we cannot measure.

- Anchor practice improvement in disciplined inquiry.

- Accelerate improvements through networked communities.

The second aspect of networked improvement communities is that the complexity of the challenge makes it very hard for individual schools to solve problems alone—it suggests working together in networks.

Some districts have successfully used improvement science to attack discrete problems including chronic absenteeism (the major predictor of dropping out), undermatching of minority students to postsecondary opportunities, and biases in disciplinary referrals in middle schools. Bryk notes Fresno Unified School District in California and the School District of the Menomonie Area in Wisconsin as examples of districts that have equipped staff members to run rapid improvement tests and regularly report on how they can get better at what they do. Both districts have experienced a cultural transformation including students taking increasing personal responsibility for advancing their own learning.

New Visions for Public Schools in New York City has supported the development of hundreds of new schools in New York City including a managed network of charter high schools that has deployed the principles of improvement to drive up graduation rates. Similarly, a grant-funded network of community colleges used the principles of improvement to increase math passing rates in developmental courses.

The Berkeley, California-based National Writing Project builds teacher capacity to improve writing. Traditionally they were what Bryk calls a "community of common concern"— a group of individuals interested in learning about how they might individually improve their instruction. Drawing on the relational strengths that they have grown across the teacher network, they are taking working as a "community of common accomplishment."

The key to the transition, says Bryk, is focusing on a specific problem and "seeing how our educational systems actually create the unsatisfactory outcomes we observe." Next comes picking important metrics of progress and building analytic infrastructure. The heart of networked improvement communities is disciplined experimentation through iterative testing of new routines and practices and tracking progress.

And then, adds Bryk, "to tackle the larger, more complex and persistent problems we confront, we join together in improvement networks." A networked improvement community within the National Writing Project was organized to focus on argument writing (a common problem identified by Common Core State Standards). "While our individual capacities may be modest, working together we can achieve much more," said Bryk.[3]

Networked improvement communities are another organized and collective research and development approach to attack complex problems. It's the opposite of a list of "proven" programs to be implemented. Like design thinking (discussed in Chapter Five), networked improvement communities take an iterative and adaptive approach to problem-solving, the kind of approach it will take to redress longstanding inequities in educational outcomes.

CONVENING LEARNING LEADERS

The New Tech Network hosts two national Leadership Summits each school year in strategic locations across the country. The convenings include "Excursions" to visit schools and explore local community-school partnerships. The goal is to create the conditions for school and district leaders to reflect upon and learn to grow their schools as learning organizations in collaboration with Network peers while capitalizing on the local landscape as a learning opportunity.

The Fall 2015 convening in Detroit, Michigan included a visit to Belleville New Tech High School to explore their literacy strategy. More unusual excursion stops included a walking tour of Detroit's Eastern Market to observe the graffiti art contributed by an international cohort of artists and to consider project-based connections. Next up was a visit to a community partner that provides student volunteer and internship opportunities. Last stop was a neighborhood urban gardening effort.

A goal of this experience was to emphasize that good project based learning takes students out into the community physically, and not just intellectually. As participants were exposed to and reflected upon the real-life projects underway in Detroit, they were asked to unpack the role of community engagement as an important component of project based learning, and assess how different approaches change, enhance, or increase such connections in their own school communities.

Participants grappled with questions such as, "What does it take to design learning opportunities like this?", "Why doesn't it happen more often?", and "What are the structures that can allow for learning opportunities like these to be the norm?"

While New Tech Network summits are bookended by excursions, the core content is immersive case studies of real school challenges from problem identification to improved student outcomes. Like the New Tech student experience, school leadership teams are immersed in applied and relevant integrated learning.

TEACHER LEADERS ACCELERATING IMPACT

Former special education teacher Seth Andrew founded Democracy Prep Public Schools in 2005 and opened his flagship middle school in Harlem the following year. By 2009, it was the highest performing school in Central Harlem and the number one public middle school in New York City. By 2016, the seventeen-school Democracy Prep network was a model of civic education and college preparation for low-income students.

Having developed one of the most important school networks in the country, Andrew learned that despite barriers of money, politics, and traditional structures, a dedicated team can open great schools that change life trajectories. The downside is that the growth of school networks is linear—about 10% annually—while the challenge is exponential.

The work of transforming existing schools, which Carnegie Foundation supports, is complex and uncertain. Developing new schools, especially with the support of experienced networks like Democracy Prep, has a good track record but is slow and expensive. The pressing issue for this sector is how to accelerate impact.

The New Tech Network faced requests from many districts interested in implementing their school model, but wanted multiple pathways to adopt and adapt New Tech practices that featured lighter supports than the traditional multi-year whole school implementation. Similar to the Summit Learning program, New Tech developed NT Teams, a faster and cheaper starting strategy that provides teacher teams with less training and coaching while still providing access to the Echo platform, the library of integrated projects, and optional professional development. NT Teams, combined with whole school implementations, serve as flexible starting points for school and district-wide transformation efforts.

Among the most encouraging innovation efforts underway by New Tech Network are multi-faceted design efforts that enable districts to spread, scale, and sustain innovation. The New Tech team has learned that scaling innovative schools requires a broad range of supports for districts to facilitate systemic change and calls for highly adaptive approaches tied to school data that assesses student growth. The 2017 NTN Student Outcomes Report offers evidence that this networked approach leads to success for diverse students in rural, urban and suburban schools.

Another effort harnessing the initiative of teacher leaders is a network of one and two-room microschools spreading across Denver, Colorado. These innovative schools provide personalized, whole-child learning with strong community connections. These tiny schools will either flourish as teacher-led schools, grow into larger schools, or see their practices adopted by their host school.

Small, teacher-powered schools have been around for 20 years, but platforms and networks are making it easier to launch and manage innovative personalized schools. It is likely that they help further efforts in accelerating impact.

DESIGNING NETWORK STRUCTURES

Most of us work and learn in networks, some formal, and many informal. There is a growing body of research about human networks, particularly those aimed at positive impact. Based on a network handbook by Peter Plastrik and Madeleine Taylor[4] and insights from network expert Curtis Ogden of the Interaction Institute for Social Change, we have compiled 10 lessons on effective network structures, and an example from education for each:

Different structures serve different purposes. A loose, multi-hub structure speeds cost-effective diffusion. The Department of Education sponsored Future Ready Schools, a loose affiliation of districts committed to forward-leaning design principles.

A centralized network based on a comprehensive school model and tight controls promotes fidelity. Success Academy is a managed network serving low-income New York City elementary students. They share their school model through a loose network, the Education Institute.

Watch the impact of dominant hubs. A dominant network hub is useful for addressing routine technical problems or supporting the execution of defined strategies. A dominant hub is often not well suited to adaptive challenges—those never experienced before—or highly varied challenges where the context for each node is different and changing. A dominant hub can impede the movement of information and resources and get in the way of the other network members developing strong relationships with each other.

The more dynamic the setting and the more differentiated the nodes, the more important it is to bring the outside in (listening to and observing clients/stakeholders). This encourages innovation and iteration at the node level, and promotes sharing across the network.

Given the size and diverse demands on urban school districts, many urban districts have adopted a portfolio strategy to leverage the power of networks.[5] Rather than attempting to develop one best practices approach, school districts like Denver Public Schools incubate and authorize charter management organizations as well as in-district "innovation school" networks.

While each network has unique learning models, tools, and professional learning experiences, all Denver schools, regardless of the form of governance, share enrollment, funding, facility, transportation, and accountability systems. This portfolio approach provides unique choices to parents and educators, allows multiple simultaneous innovations in a dynamic system, and avoids the problems associated with a dominant hub.

Build strong connections. What makes networks adaptive is a strong connected periphery. Pushing responsibility out to the edges is what helps networks survive and thrive. Many networks are flipping a top-down and center-focused orientation to seeing the periphery as norm.

Connecting the edges starts with shared values. NAF is a network of 675 career academy members in 461 high schools. They share a small school structure, a core career-themed curriculum, and the NAFTrack Certification system which combines college and career-ready skills and dispositions. "In building and sustaining the NAF network, comprised of education, business, and community leaders, each member values the importance of strengthening connections and sharing resources, and have witnessed preliminary relationships becoming longstanding partnerships over time," said former Executive Vice President Andrew Rothstein.

Shared infrastructure is also important to productive connections. Across NAF, the myNAFTrack platform connects members including students, alumni, and certified hiring partners. The platform and certification system make contributions simple, specific, and meaningful.

Invest in shifting structures. As networks evolve, their shifting structures require different kinds of care. Each of these tasks is about developing connectivity, alignment, and production—but within very different structural contexts.

After 20 years of decentralized operation the KIPP network invested in a curriculum, more as a resource than requirement, to better support teachers and students and partners with districts to scale impact.

With more than 50 schools in Texas, IDEA Public Schools taps the expertise of a national advisory board to identify and launch personalized learning experiments across the network. These experiments test instructional strategies, software, schedules, and structures.

The Learning Assembly is a network of school support networks, including Citizen Schools, Digital Promise, Highlander Institute, New York iZone, LearnLaunch, LEAP Innovations, and the Silicon Valley Education Foundation. They have supported personalized learning tests in 195 schools. These tests help schools make informed decisions about strategies and tools.

Make the network do the work. Like self-checkout at the store, pumping your own gasoline, and automated tellers at the bank, automation often pushes work back to the end user. Strong networks create conditions for self-development and co-creation. Rather than viewing members as passive extractors, they ask them to collaborate to produce value. For example, teachers in the New Tech Network create and share project-based units.

Let connections flow to value. Rather than gatekeeping, strong networks encourage co-creation and allow popular nodes to attract and share resources. They avoid doing things that members don't find valuable, and value contributions before credentials.

Rather than hiring consultants to develop an elementary school model, the New Tech Network encouraged Katherine Smith Elementary in San Jose to join and supported their innovative work, making it the basis for the network elementary model. Other elementary schools quickly followed, and now there are more than 20 elementary schools learning together in the New Tech Network.

Use variation to strengthen a network. A network's ability to create adaptive capacity depends crucially on assembling specialized competencies among its members. For example, Leadership Public Schools, a small high school network in Oakland, California, uses a distributed and collaborative innovation strategy—each school takes a part of the plan and develops a new capacity in close coordination with other schools.

Strong networks encourage difference but also make connections across governance and geographic boundaries. Schools in the New Tech Network share a common focus on project based learning, but many schools have unique missions—they are urban and rural, STEM-focused and arts-focused, magnet schools and dropout recovery schools.

It's a network-to-network world. If you can weave the clusters together, the network you are building will grow faster and have more immediate connectivity and capacity. One capacity-building example is the Deeper Learning Equity Fellowship, a partnership between Big Picture Learning and the Internationals Network—a network serving networks.

Promote equity and diversity. We all carry implicit bias and it can seep into and become part of our networks. Strong networks counter bias by encouraging interaction and design thinking—which starts with empathy

Members of the Remake Learning Network in Pittsburgh—some 250 schools, libraries, universities, startups, and museums—pursue equity through a shared agenda of innovative teaching and learning. New thinking comes from the meeting of different fields, experience, and perspectives.

Keep plans flexible. Networks tend to plan two things: projects they will undertake, one after another, and the development of the network as a whole. Districts and networks use projects to distribute and develop leadership while carrying out a change agenda.

These lessons suggest a set of core skills for working in networks: inquiry, design thinking, cultivating trust, making connections, creating safe spaces for differences, and supporting self-organizing and co-creation.

The promise of networks is that whole is greater than the sum of its parts. The prospect of improving American public education one school at a time is agonizingly slow. This raises all sorts of questions about equity and lost generations of students, while we work to improve one little red schoolhouse at a time. Networks offer the promise of accelerating the learning and improvement of schools, reducing the risks, and thus improvement in student outcomes, to a far greater degree than any single school working in isolation might reasonably expect.

In the context of networks, then, the individual posture and character of the organizations that collectively come together to form a network matters a great deal. Even in the context of a single organization or school, where individuals see one another and work together every day, it is hard work to foster the disciplined, deep, and ongoing practice of collaborative learning and improvement. To do so in a network (where the context of relationship building is constrained by limited opportunities for face-to-face interaction) becomes increasingly difficult. If the individual organizations within a network do not have any exposure to and orientation around the work of improvement, it will be exponentially more difficult to bring forth network-like behavior, and the disciplined, deep, and ongoing practice of collaborative learning that can happen across multiple schools or organizations. Learning organizations are essential to realizing the power of learning networks.

NOTES

1. http://www.gettingsmart.com/wp-content/uploads/2016/05/Singapore-American-School.pdf
2. https://www.carnegiefoundation.org/wp-content/uploads/2017/04/Carnegie_Bryk_Summit_17_Keynote.pdf
3. Personal email from September 19, 2017.
4. http://networkimpact.org/downloads/NetGainsHandbookVersion1.pdf
5. http://www.gettingsmart.com/2017/04/competitive-coherent-creative-21st-century-school-district

DYNAMIC NETWORKS

Picking the Right Structure for Scaled Impact

Teachers nationwide are working hard to personalize learning and new tools that can help, but in many schools teachers do not benefit from a fully aligned system designed for their success. Personalized learning models are challenging to build and manage. Competency-based progressions add complexity and require a high degree of team coordination and new forms of student, teacher, and school support.

Developing or adapting platform tools to a learning model is a big technical challenge. Add talent development demands and you have a trifecta that is daunting for even the most experienced teams.

By providing design principles, curriculum materials, technology tools, and professional learning opportunities, networks make it easier to create a good new school or transform an existing school. As a result, school networks will play an increasingly important role in bringing quality to scale. While a few schools with heroic leadership can function in the long term on their own, most schools should join a network or operate within a network—or a district that operates like a network.

School networks are one of the most important innovations in the modern era of US K–12 education. They have boosted achievement levels and graduation rates and expanded options in communities that need them most.

Through the Achievement School District, the state of Tennessee enlisted the help of five national school networks and incubated seven local networks to support the lowest performing schools in the state. Since then, the 85 schools supported by the ASD have shown promising improvement.[1]

From rural communities like Cherry Valley, Arkansas to big districts like El Paso, Texas, school districts have forged partnerships with the New Tech Network to create engaging schools in neighborhoods that have struggled for decades to create quality options.

The advent of personalized learning makes school models even more important. Like precision medicine, personalized learning will require sophisticated platforms and large-scale informatics infrastructure. In education, informatics infrastructure is most likely to be developed by large school networks with a commitment to a shared learning model, assessment system, and platform.

ALL OF US: LAUNCHING PRECISION MEDICINE

The National Institutes of Health (NIH) launched All of Us (http://allofus.nih.gov), a study including at least one million volunteers who provide genetic data, biological samples, and other information about their health. To encourage open data sharing, participants will be able to access their health information during the study, as well as research that uses their data. Researchers will use this dataset to study a large range of diseases, with the goals of better predicting disease risk, understanding how diseases occur, and finding improved diagnosis and treatment strategies. The program infrastructure is a network of U.S. industry and university partners, a prototype model for precision medicine.

Figure 8.1 compares six types of networks ranging from voluntary associations around design principles (loose design and loose control) to managed networks (tight design and tight control). The first bullet is the key characteristic, the second bullet includes network examples, and the last two bullets are examples of funders and advocates supporting the strategy.

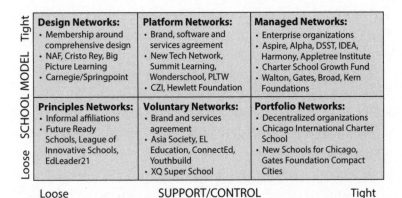

Figure 8.1 Network types, examples, and funders/advocates

Managed networks: Charter management organizations (CMOs) have grown to more than 2,800 schools (about 40% of all charters). There are more than 50 high-quality, scaled charter networks—most of which share a learning model, professional learning supports, and increasingly, platform tools. A representative sample follows.

Harmony Public Schools has 54 STEM-focused schools in Texas. Idea Public Schools is a network of 61 blended schools in south Texas. Aspire Public Schools serves 16,000 students in 40 schools in California and Tennessee. DSST Public Schools serves 10,500 students in 11 Denver schools.

Several new charter networks have innovative learning models. Alpha Public Schools is a small blended learning leader in San Jose, California. Thrive Public Schools in San Diego, California combines personalized, project-based, and social emotional learning.

Spurred by charter school competition Alex Magaña led the successful turnaround of Grant Beacon Middle School in Denver, Colorado. District leadership asked Alex to create a network to replicate his success in other struggling schools. In the fall of 2016, the Beacon Network opened a second school. As Innovation Schools within the Denver Public School system, both schools have charter-like autonomy. Teaching and learning at each school is driven by a focus on critical thinking, personalization through blended learning, character development, and extended day enrichment opportunities.[2]

Another early in-district network is Mesita Elementary in El Paso, Texas. A multi-campus dual language leader, Mesita Elementary spearheads the district's commitment to dual language through a partnership with University of Texas El Paso, which supports 250 pre-service teachers.[3]

Wildflower Schools is a growing national network of Montessori microschools. Founded in 2014, Wildflower developed an open-source model that helps teacher-leaders to create new schools. Each teacher-leader at each Wildflower school serves on the board of at least one other Wildflower school, creating a community of schools that are linked by both a shared philosophy and a network of shared relationships.

AppleTree Institute is a managed network of 10 early learning charter schools in Washington, D.C. (the only jurisdiction to extend charter legislation to early learning). The Every Child Ready curriculum was developed with federal i3 grant funding. It includes curriculum (what to teach), professional development (how to teach) and assessment (how do we know if it worked?). AppleTree is a good example of using policy innovations and grant opportunities to scale impact.[4]

In business, these vertically integrated networks would be called enterprise systems—organizations committed to common processes, systems, and metrics. Some small districts operate as managed networks.[5]

Platform networks: As discussed in Chapter Six, Summit Public Schools is both a managed network of innovative West Coast secondary schools and, with support from the Chan Zuckerberg Initiative, a platform network—Summit Learning, which makes its learning platform and support services available to more than 330 school teams.

The New Tech Network, discussed extensively in this book, is also a platform network with a shared project-based K–12 learning model, a learning platform, and professional learning opportunities.

Teton Science Schools are small, community connected schools in Idaho and Wyoming. The K–12 schools, field education programs, and graduate school in this network are the best example of place-based education—a learner-centered approach that prioritizes student engagement with the world around them. Their proposed Place Schools Program is a network of personalized rural microschools.

AltSchool is a venture-based San Francisco startup that manages a small network of elementary microschools and is beginning to allow partner schools to gain access to its personalized learning platform. "We are a project-based school. We use a variety of assessments to understand where kids are," said Colleen Broderick, VP for Pedagogy and Research. She said they "are doubling down on how kids understand their own potential" as well as "enable[ing] them to be changemakers in their own community."[6] While leaving lots of options, Broderick is working on articulating "a learning flow" so that teachers don't always have to figure out what's next. The platform doesn't require a single learning model but adds value to schools committed to cultivating learner agency through whole-child, personalized learning.

Wonderschool is a Los Angeles-based "preschool-in-a-box" platform that makes it easy for any household to launch and market a preschool. Similarly, CottageClass, a Manhattan startup, makes it easy to launch and market full or part-time microschool learning opportunities.

In 2014, RAMTEC, a program of the Tri-Rivers Career Center in Marion, Ohio, successfully certified high school students on the two leading robotics systems. The state provided grants allowing the program to be expanded to 22 other sites, and providing access to high school and college students as well as adult learners. As a result, hundreds of young people in Ohio are in high-wage jobs with continuing education opportunities—a technical work-and-learn ladder.

While not a full school model, Project Lead The Way (PLTW) provides science, math, engineering and technology (STEM) curriculum on a learning platform (Canvas) with associated equipment, implementation support, live classroom support, and professional learning opportunities. The Indianapolis nonprofit encourages participating teachers to share best practices and inspiration.

Advancement Via Individual Determination, better known as AVID, is a San Diego nonprofit organization that provides a comprehensive college readiness system to about 6,000 schools. Perhaps most importantly, AVID helps to create a college-going culture in schools. "When teachers are engaged, owning common practices and beliefs, and trained fellow by colleagues, it changes the culture," said CEO Sandy Husk. Member schools stay up to date with AVID Weekly, local and regional trainings, summer institutes, and a national conference in December. AVID is becoming a true platform network as they digitize their curriculum and resources.[7]

More than 9,500 high schools and colleges offer the Cisco Networking Academy. They share courseware, professional learning, and certification exams across the network. Over one million students participate each year.

Several digital curriculum vendors have become platform networks. Apex Learning provides secondary education courses, tutorials, implementation support, and professional development on a proprietary platform. Fuel Education provides online secondary courses through the Peak platform. Edgenuity offers K–12 curriculum, professional development, and virtual instruction.

Design networks: These member networks are voluntary associations of schools focused around design principles and support services. All of them benefit from philanthropic contributions.

Internship-focused Big Picture Learning partner schools share a well-documented student-centered learning model. Big Picture Learning supports 52 US schools and 39 international partner schools. Edvisions is a similar student-centered, upper Midwestern network with 37 affiliated schools.

The National Academy Foundation (NAF) is the largest and one of the oldest networks in the country, with 675 career academy members in 461 high schools serving over

100,000 students. They share a small school structure, and a core career-themed curriculum focused on one of five growing industries: finance, hospitality and tourism, information technology, engineering, and health sciences. The NAFTrack

ACTON ACADEMY

A small but audacious school in Austin, Texas claims that, "Each person who enters our doors will find a calling that will change the world."

Acton Academy is a small private K–12 school that, through a lightweight franchising approach, has expanded to more than 80 locations in eight countries. Some new schools only consist of 10 students, while more mature locations are nearing a maximum size of 120 young people.

There are 5,300 applications from parents around the world wanting to open one for their own children.

Acton schools use Socratic questions to hone deep thinking, as well as peer teaching, apprenticeships for real world learning, and online learning for mastering the basics of reading, grammar, and math. Hands-on projects designed with game theory incentives deliver opportunities for young people to dig into the arts, sciences, world history, and economics by solving real problems, analyzing moral dilemmas, making difficult decisions, persuading audiences to action, creating innovative opportunities for the world, resolving personal conflicts, and even making and managing money.

The ultimate goal, though, is to learn how to learn, learn how to do, and learn how to be, so that each person will find a calling and change the world. Each person who graduates from an Acton Academy will be equipped to master the next step in their life plan with gusto—whether it be attending a fine university, taking a gap year to travel, or starting a business.

Certification system integrates college and career-ready skills and dispositions in a comprehensive and cumulative system that combines coursework at school and workplace observations with supervisor feedback.

The Mastery Collaborative is a network of 42 New York City public middle and high schools implementing competency-based learning. They share design principles and technical assistance, and attend quarterly meetings and summer institutes. "We are beginning to orient teaching and learning in a completely different way—designing learning arcs that end in demonstrations of independent mastery—as compared to the conventional system of delivering curriculum and instruction," explained John Duval, who supports the network.[8] He added that they are developing a "handbook that is specific enough that teachers can understand what instruction looks like in the classroom when students are empowered, when there is transparency, and when the primary focus is on skill-building." The network is a good example of an in-district network piloting a comprehensive package of innovations.

Voluntary networks: With a bit more site flexibility, voluntary school networks share design principles and professional development services (but not a platform).

With roots in expeditions and Outward Bound, EL Education has 152 schools with a recent focus on curriculum. Executive Director Scott Hartl thinks of their work as the "software" for the network. "We're not an operator," said Hartl. "We're the software—the guts of an academic program, the adult learning, the blueprint for culture and climate."[9] With digital curriculum updates, EL will emerge as an important curriculum network with content, platform, and professional learning services. EL is also launching a leadership development program focusing on positional coaching with the view that "leadership is not a person, it's a function," one that is spread across a school ecosystem.

Internationals Network for Public Schools serves recently arrived immigrants in 27 schools and academies in eight states and the District of Columbia. In addition to supporting schools in the network, the organization provides consulting services to districts to improve outcomes for English Language Learners. Asia Society's International Studies Schools Network (ISSN) has 34 schools in eight states that share a focus on four global competencies: investigating the world beyond their immediate environment, recognizing perspectives, communicating ideas, and taking action. The ISSN school design includes common vision, mission and culture; shared student learning outcomes; organization and governance structures; community partnerships; a cycle of professional development; and a framework of curriculum, instruction, and assessment.

Urban Assembly serves over 9,000 students through 21 student-centered public middle and high schools, including seven career and technical schools and three all-girls schools.

YouthBuild is a network of 260 high school programs in 46 states aimed at boosting employability in building-related trades and leadership development. (These design and voluntary networks received early support from the Bill & Melinda Gates Foundation.)

In 2006, with over $100 million in funding from the James Irvine Foundation, Berkeley, California nonprofit ConnectEd developed and launched Linked Learning, a comprehensive approach combining rigorous academics, career-based learning in class, work-based learning, and integrated student supports. Nine California districts, ranging from tiny Porterville Unified School District to giant Los Angeles Unified, won big grants to implement the package of reforms. Schools shared ConnectEd Studios, a digital environment that supports implementation and assessment of student work. SRI found that students in well-implemented pathways were more likely to graduate from high school, were less likely to drop out, and earned, on average, more credits.[10] After the initial grant-funded initiative ended in 2015, ConnectEd began working with districts in other states, sponsored by grants and fees.

The Center for Advanced Professional Studies (CAPS) provides discovery, works skills, and professions-based learning to students in the Blue Valley School District in suburban Kansas City. In a lightweight voluntary network, the program has been replicated and adapted by more than 74 districts through the CAPS Network.

LRNG is a national network of out-of-school learning providers in nine partner cities. Learners complete playlists of experiences—some online, some in person—to earn badges, a publicly shareable digital credential that provides evidence of learning. LRNG is becoming a national platform network; think of it as Uber for learning experiences, as it continues to add cities, providers, and learners.

Principles networks: Loose networks around shared principles can be scaled quickly and inexpensively, but with no platform and limited professional learning they are plagued with big variations in implementation.

Over 3,100 districts have committed to the principles of Future Ready Schools, a project launched 2014 as a partnership between the U.S. Department of Education and the Alliance for Excellent Education. Support includes regional convenings, tools, and resources.

EdLeader21, part of Battelle for Kids, is a national network of over 200 school district leaders with shared interest in deeper learning outcomes. Members gain access to resources to support integration of the 4Cs—critical thinking, communication, collaboration, and creativity.

The Tarrant Institute at the University of Vermont works with 22 schools in the state in supporting their move towards "a tech-rich, student-centered model of young adolescent education."

Portfolio networks: As a scaling strategy, the smallest category is portfolio networks. Like Chicago International Charter School, they are diverse school models that share school supervision and backend support systems.

Most districts operate as portfolio networks with a partially defined school model (perhaps a shared schedule and calendar), graduation requirements, and some curricular and support services. Unlike scratch-build networks, the decision-making framework in school districts is often a murky, negotiated settlement that evolved over years of practice and policy. These idiosyncratic management systems makes it challenging to create role and goal clarity—a key to performance and satisfaction.

WHICH SCALING STRATEGY IS BEST?

As shown in Figure 8.2, each category of school network offers distinct advantages and challenges. Managed networks are expensive and challenging to build, but deliver the most consistent quality. A focus on execution in managed networks can stifle innovation and creativity.[11]

SCHOOL MODEL	Tight	**Design Networks:** + Open to innovation + Tight on key variables, loose others – Quality varies	**Platform Networks:** + Scalable quality + Microschool opportunity – Challenge to build – Whole school models slow & expensive to scale	**Managed Networks:** + Implementation fidelity yields quality at scale – Challenge to build – Can repress innovation – Slow & expensive to scale
	Loose	**Principles Networks:** + Low cost to scale – Low fidelity	**Voluntary Networks:** + Flexible, moderate cost – Low/moderate fidelity	**Portfolio Networks:** + Open to adaptation/themes + Provide options – Moderate fidelity
		Loose	SUPPORT/CONTROL	Tight

Figure 8.2 Advantages and disadvantages of network types

Design networks and principles networks are low-cost ways to share the success of a school model. Networks like EdLeader21 (part of Battelle for Kids) serve as a professional learning community for system heads. These low-cost affiliates can be dynamic places to share best practices, but they can also lose their driving energy and collapse (like the Coalition of Essential Schools). The downside to these networks is wide-ranging implementation fidelity.

With technology advances, platform networks are becoming the most attractive option for scaling a learning model. Like managed networks, platform networks have relied on expensive and slow new school development. As shown in Figure 8.3, Summit Public Schools, a charter management organization, created Summit Learning, a platform network free to teacher teams that apply to gain access to the learning model, platform, and professional learning. Similarly, venture-backed AltSchool began as a managed network but has shifted focus to a subscription-based platform network available to partner schools.

Like the New Tech Network, Acton Academy was developed and is being expanded as a platform network. As shown

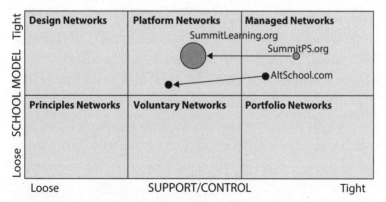

Figure 8.3 Network models: Migrating to expand impact

141

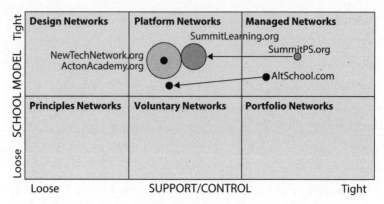

Figure 8.4 Network models: Growing platform networks

in Figure 8.4, Acton replication is a lightweight franchising approach where "owners" (who must have children in the school) pay a small fee to join the network and use the Acton brand. They agree to a common set of practices and they all install Nest cameras that create a network-wide view of what's happening in Acton schools. There are more than 90 Acton Academies with a fifth located internationally including South America and Malaysia Owners freely share best practices online. Founder Jeff Sandefer said he picks up about three ideas a week from colleagues across the network.[12]

As shown in Figure 8.5, PLTW and AVID are examples of comprehensive programs that include courses, curriculum, professional learning, and collaboration opportunities. Both programs continue to move more of their resources online, becoming more like platform networks in the process (which will cause them to move further up on the chart in Figure 8.5, towards Summit Learning). If these nonprofits take advantage of the two-way interaction and potential for co-creation,

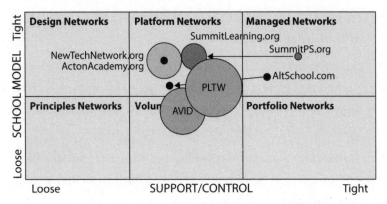

Figure 8.5 Network models: Growing curriculum networks

both networks could become even more dynamic and improve teacher experience and student learning.

NETWORK TIPS

Part Two has illustrated examples of powerful learning and made the case that these kinds of experiences are more likely to happen when educators work together in networks. To conclude this section, we offer the following tips:

- *Teacher:* Identify networks of interest, then locate and visit local member schools.

- *Teacher leader:* Start (or join) a professional learning community to leverage your impact.

- *School leader:* If you are in a district where you are required to use specific tools and services (like a portfolio network), check out the design networks as potential support systems for a coherent learning model.

- *Successful school leader:* Propose a multi-campus expansion or in-district network.

- *Superintendents:* Check out the platform networks as potential partners for struggling schools or underserved segments. Managed networks could become portfolio partners (which is discussed further in Chapter Ten).

- *Curriculum directors:* Consider curriculum networks with online content and resources, and professional learning opportunities.

- *Provider:* If you built a tool or platform, networks can help bring it to scale with high fidelity use. Propose a pilot project to get some quality user data.

Part Three is about taking powerful learning experiences to scale and the levers of leadership, network strategy, governance, and public policy.

NOTES

1. http://achievementschooldistrict.org/wp-content/uploads/2015/11/The-Achievement-School-District-Lessons-from-Tennessee-UPDATE.pdf
2. http://www.gettingsmart.com/2017/02/kepner-keeps-true-innovation-model
3. http://www.gettingsmart.com/2016/07/dual-language-education-for-equity-economic-development
4. http://www.gettingsmart.com/2016/04/dc-extends-performance-contracting-k-12-pre-k-residential-adult-ed
5. See a list of 10 districts that operate as networks at http://www.gettingsmart.com/2017/01/how-to-create-experiences-and-scale-environments-that-change-lives
6. http://www.gettingsmart.com/2017/05/altschool-designing-the-future-learning

7. http://www.gettingsmart.com/2017/05/getting-smart-podcast-avid-an-integrated-approach-to-college-readiness
8. https://www.inacol.org/news/talking-equity-with-john-duval
9. http://www.gettingsmart.com/2017/03/scott-hartl-on-growing-schools-that-foster-wonderful-ideas
10. https://www.sri.com/work/publications/taking-stock-california-linked-learning-district-initiative-seventh-year
11. http://www.gettingsmart.com/2016/10/on-balancing-improvement-innovation
12. http://www.gettingsmart.com/2017/04/getting-smart-podcast-acton-academy-building-a-student-centered-school-and-global-network

PART THREE

NAVIGATING THE FUTURE . . . STARTING NOW

LEADERSHIP

From Compliance to Agreement Crafting

"**D**eeper learning outcomes are good for all kids," said Superintendent Kathy Gomez. "They promote agency, self-confidence, and lifelong learning with a sense of 'I can figure this out' whether that be a college pathway or a career access point."

Gomez leads the Evergreen Elementary School District, which serves both affluent and high-need neighborhoods in San Jose, California and poses a range of challenges to meet the needs of all students. Evergreen is also home to Katherine Smith Elementary (featured in Chapter Five), where the majority of students are English Language Learners and live in or near poverty. As the district's school design partner, New Tech Network has worked closely with Evergreen educators to advance their commitment to provide deeper learning for all students. This district vision is causing big shifts as schools move from traditional structures to student-centered, innovative models.

"For Evergreen, implementing a project based learning instructional approach in conjunction with the cultural foundations of trust, respect, and responsibility is how they ensure all kids leave their system with the social and academic self-confidence that comes with attaining deeper learning outcomes," said Gomez.

For school districts seeking deeper learning experiences for their students, Gomez notes that organizational shifts are often more cultural than they are technical. "Teachers teach the way they were taught," she explained. "It's too easy for teachers and administrators to do what they've always done because they've always done it that way." Implementing technical shifts—new technology, new curriculum, and new space—without addressing the existing culture will likely render those changes are less effective.

A cultural shift requires leaders to be vulnerable with staff and partners. According to Gomez, "you have to be comfortable being completely honest and vulnerable in airing your dirty laundry." A spirit of openness can help build trust with staff, so that they believe they have the freedom to change.

Gomez gives school leaders the space and time to choose a new focus for their school that will best meet the needs of their students. She has helped to clear the path for this work by changing the way accountability is discussed within the district. "We're spending a lot of time talking about outcomes instead of [state] test scores," says Gomez. Balancing autonomy with clarity of purpose goes a long way in establishing trust within the larger system.

"Parents are critical to school success and are vocal when they support or don't support a particular direction," Gomez said. "Making sure parents understand the 'why' of the shift is essential." If children are happy and learning, parents are generally happy, but there are still "many parents who are uncomfortable with non-traditional learning environments. They may be intrigued by the non-traditional, but are a little hesitant to apply it to 'their' kids." Yet as Gomez notes, "That's okay! Slow and steady wins the race!"

Sustained rather than heroic leadership is key. Gomez notes that it takes time for changes to become institutionalized; despite a traditional district structure, "topics of conversation emerge from the front lines rather than from the top." District officials introduce questions rather than solutions, though Gomez remains hopeful for the work ahead: "We are working to build leadership capacity and help our leadership team and teachers think about why they are doing what they are doing and ultimately help them tap into the passion they had when they entered the profession."

"We picked New Tech Network because of the flexibility that NTN allows—no rigid model that must be strictly implemented," she said. "The customized and tailored support with our Instruction team was critical as we seek to spread deeper learning through our district." However, she suggests, it would not be possible to receive such strategic support if the district had not fully revealed their candid assessment of their needs early on in the work together.

Change at this scale is never easy. So why engage in district redesign in the first place? "Because it's the right thing to do," Gomez explained, "if we want our kids to be prepared for their future."

LEADING FOR DEEPER LEARNING: TIPS FROM EVERGREEN SUPERINTENDENT KATHY GOMEZ

- **Leadership:** Be willing to be vulnerable.
- **Culture:** The shift to deeper learning is more cultural than technical.
- **Trust:** Full adoption requires trust among staff so they so that they believe they have the freedom to change.
- **Time:** It takes time for changes to become institutionalized.
- **Voice:** Develop leadership across the system by incorporating the voices of principals, teachers, and students into the development of new practices.
- **Partners:** Pick partners that share your vision and values.

PERSONALIZED LEARNING FOR TEACHERS

Microcredentials are a digital form of certification that indicates when a person has demonstrated competency in a specific skill set. As a progress tracking and signaling system, microcredentials are gaining traction in education since they offer a promising approach to personalized, competency-based professional learning.[1]

"The beauty of the microcredential is that it gives teachers the experience we're hoping they are giving their students. It's not just a seat time requirement, it requires a student demonstration of learning, artifacts of learning, and student reflection," said Kettle Moraine Superintendent Patricia DeKlotz.[2]

The community expects personalized learning for all students, said DeKlotz. But she notes that many teachers were not prepared to deliver personalized literacy skills across the curriculum. For example, math teachers received zero instruction on literacy strategies. Rather than requiring all their teachers to attend a class, DeKlotz encouraged high school leaders to develop literacy microcredentials.

Leaders of the Kettle Moraine School District (west of Milwaukee, Wisconsin) are committed to teacher professionalism in the microcredential process. Rather than inflicting a compliance culture, microcredentials reward teacher leadership and alignment with district initiatives. And compared to traditional professional development, DeKlotz believes this approach is far more robust because it considers the impact on learning in the classroom. "It's been very powerful in our district," said DeKlotz noting that 80% of teachers have earned microcredentials since the program started, making them eligible for extra pay for demonstrating new skills.

Beginning in 2012, DeKlotz solicited plans for four small personalized, project-based charter schools to be housed inside existing facilities. Three high school programs launched with two teachers and about 40 students. These innovative microschools were another example of a pull innovation strategy (incentives and opportunities) rather than a push strategy (universal compliance requirements).

Kettle Moraine is an active member of a national network of 93 districts called the League of Innovative Schools, a network of school districts launched by Digital Promise in 2014. Reaching more than 3.3 million students, League members are peer-vetted and sign a membership charter signaling commitment to student learning, networking, and knowledge-sharing. The League connects district leaders with leading entrepreneurs and researchers, encouraging them to serve as test beds for new tools and practices and to connect with like-minded districts to attack big challenges.

"In addition to building great connections with superintendents from all over the country, I've found participating in the League's working groups to be a great learning vehicle, for me and for district staff," said DeKlotz. "In particular, the competency-based learning efforts have resulted in each member contributing playlist content." She added, "Rather than discovering this work in isolation we are building a playlist that districts can consider, so that they can learn from and further build on the pioneering work of others."

When creating new teaching and learning practices in an exciting but not clearly defined space like competency-based learning or teacher microcredentials, DeKlotz finds that being part of the League provides access to research, resources and peers who are grappling with similar challenges. She enjoys immersing herself in host district initiatives, and values opportunities to do just that at the biannual meetings.

"The enduring value is that by participating in the working groups, I am able to play a clearer, more active role in moving

LEADING FOR DEEP LEARNING: TIPS FROM PATRICIA DEKLOTZ

- Use innovative incentives that encourage aligned action around common goals
- Support the same kind of learning for teachers that you want for students
- Give people the tools they need to do the work
- Join networks that support your collective goals

from district vision to execution, and this ultimately leads to far more effective and meaningful student experiences and outcomes," added DeKlotz.

Supported by the Open Badge Standard developed by Mozilla and digital badging technology, microcredentials provide educators with concrete validation of their learning that can be used as a type of currency in professional learning. Digital Promise hosts over 280 different microcredentials.

USER-CENTERED AGILE DESIGN

Dr. Eric Tucker is developing Brooklyn LAB, a network of secondary schools that send low-income students from Brooklyn to college prepared to thrive. "At LAB, we believe that learning experiences should meet students where they are, engage them deeply in inquiry and mastery, and tailor challenges in a dynamic, personal manner," said Tucker.

Brooklyn LAB consists of two blended middle schools and a high school that, like Summit Public Schools, is a good example of a team simultaneously developing a next-generation learning environment and platform. And like Summit, they are using two scaling strategies—a managed network and a platform network.

LAB embraces expanded definitions of student success. "We are developing and pursuing novel approaches to establish learning goals that are both broad and deep, and also span academic, cognitive, and social-emotional aims," said Tucker. They champion the MyWays Framework from Next Generation Learning Challenges, a foundation-sponsored project that has supported more than 150 new innovative secondary schools.

Like Summit's outcome framework, MyWays builds on David Conley's work[3] and codifies the key competencies to postsecondary success:

- **Content Knowledge:** Subject area knowledge and organizing concepts essential for academic and real-life applications.

- **Creative Know-How:** Skills and abilities to analyze complex problems and construct solutions in real-life situations.

- **Habits of Success:** Behaviors and practices that enable students to own their learning and cultivate personal effectiveness.

- **Wayfinding Abilities:** Knowledge and capacity to successfully navigate college, career, and life opportunities and choices.

Brooklyn LAB was designed through a user-centered, agile process informed by students, parents, and stakeholders. In the first phase, a transformation team captures user stories to define the Why (values, purpose, principles) and How (behavior, language, roles, and tasks). In phase two, the design is enacted through pilots and testing. Lots of conversations help recognize what's what working and what's not. Phase three is an ongoing operation with distributed leadership, and a focus on failing fast and short cycle innovation. It's important to remain open to feedback to keep the design dynamic.[4]

About four of ten LAB students have complex needs. By blending high-dose tutoring (about two hours daily from teaching fellows) and adaptive technology, teachers are able to create learning experience that reflect each student's interests and needs.

"School leadership and data are inextricably tied, in part because actionable evidence enables educators who are urgent about getting the job done to demand excellence of themselves and others," said Tucker:

> Operational, instructional, and assessment data allow leaders who are willing to learn (and humble enough to own when something is not working) to use evidence to inform effective academic systems; achieve consistent behavior and cultural norms; coach and develop exceptional teachers; refine college ready programs; and optimize meaningful learning time....We seek to reengineer school to become a learning-based rather than a seat time-based system through a dynamic learning-centered culture. Mastery learning rests on scoring rubrics, performance measures, standards grading, and progress reports—all of which depend on data.[5]

In order to provide LAB students with timely and customized feedback on their academic progress, the LAB team uses the Cortex platform from InnovateEdu, a New York nonprofit led by Eric's wife, Erin Mote. Built on the Ed-Fi data standard with support from the Michael and Susan Dell Foundation, the Cortex platform is highly configurable and is used by a growing number of districts and networks.

Developing a custom competency-based blended learning platform is something that most networks and districts should avoid, but the LAB-Cortex team is talented and experienced. Erin is a serious technologist who previously built a global broadband coalition for USAID. Dr. Tucker has a doctorate in social measurement from Oxford.

Together, they are using the slow growth of a managed network to show what is possible and the rapid adoption of a next-generation platform to achieve scaled impact. Brooklyn Lab plans to serve 2,200 mostly low-income Brooklyn students of color by 2020, when there will be more than ten times as many learners on the Cortex platform.

In 2016, Brooklyn Lab High School was one of 10 schools to receive $10 million grants from XQ: The Super School Project, which called on educators, students, parents, and community leaders to rethink high school in America.[6]

LEADING FOR DEEPER LEARNING: TIPS FROM ERIN MOTE AND ERIC TUCKER

- **An innovation mindset is key.** Today's world requires a mindset that emphasizes effort, initiative and collaborative.
- **User-centered design** is an ongoing commitment to listen to stakeholders
- **Agile development** is a commitment to testing quickly, and failing forward
- **Developing** a school model and platform simultaneously is challenging but can result in alignment around innovative practices. Helping organizations collaborate with their own unique talent and funding is often the best approach.
- **Innovating and executing** at high levels simultaneously requires a series of short-term agreements that clarify roles and goals for staff members and partners.

PROJECT-BASED LEADERSHIP

The best way to manage an innovation and improvement agenda is to break it into a connected series of projects and launch them in phases. Projects can be managed by emerging leaders—anyone in the organization who has expressed the interest and ability to handle broader responsibilities. Managing projects can be a great way to practice facilitation and leadership skills.

PROJECT MANAGEMENT BASICS

Project plans should include:

- **Clear goals** and well-defined deliverables
- **Timeline** with major milestones, team meetings, and scheduled sponsor reviews
- **Staffing** estimates for internal and external resources (especially paid contractors)
- **Budget** including discretionary budget and allocated time
- **Dependencies** with other projects or policies

Project roles include:

- **Executive sponsor:** Owns the outcome and can approve a change in the budget or timeline
- **Project manager:** Responsible for team effectiveness and final deliverables
- **Team member:** Contributes to team goal, and makes requested contributions
- **Advisor:** Internal or external resource providing project-related advice
- **Contractor:** Paid advisor with specific deliverables (e.g., develop and conduct a survey)

Projects can be staffed by people internal and external to the organization. Add people to the project team if they bring a required skill or perspective. If you want broader input, hold focus groups, conduct surveys, or interview people.

"It is a very cool way to spread the message about managing a 21st-century workflow in the organization, and resets the thinking of the adults to be aligned to the instructional shifts tied to project based learning implementations," said David Haglund, former deputy superintendent in Santa Ana Unified School District (and now superintendent in Pleasanton Unified School District). Haglund provided five examples of using projects to execute strategy and develop leaders[7]:

- **Kim Garcia, Curriculum Specialist,** was charged with developing the Advanced Learning Academy's academic program. She was given a huge amount of freedom and support to "build the school," and has since become the school's first principal. That school expands into high school in the fall as an early college program and will share space with Santa Ana College.

- **Wes Kriesel, Program Specialist,** was charged with developing new hybrid courses for high school students. He recruited a team to tackle that work and has been engaging crowd-sourcing and other innovative strategies to drive the work flow. They have used blogging and "live" community sessions to engage a wider set of stakeholders in the development process.

- **Daniel Allen, Executive Director,** was charged with coordinating the work of district management team members to address six "problems of practice" identified during a student panel at the annual manager's symposium. Those groups worked collaboratively to address issues related to growth mindsets, personalized learning plans, the use of technology to support personalization, expanding access to meaningful extracurricular programs, critical thinking, and restorative practices.

- **Suzie Lopez, Community Relations Specialist,** was charged with resetting the District's image in the community and improving efforts to "tell our story." She and a team of teachers and administrators worked to promote school choice by helping principals brand and market their schools in ways that were meaningful to the community. The School Choice Faire in October 2016 drew in several thousand community members to a festive event held in Downtown Santa Ana. The City closed off three blocks for the day and every school hosted booths and highlighted student performers at a central stage.

- **Mark Chavez, Director of Food Services,** heard students' frustrations about food quality during student Local Control and Accountability Plan (LCAP) sessions and responded by creating a food tasting event, where vendors were able to share their recipes, and students and parents voted on what to add to the school lunch menu.

Each of these projects was identified in the district's state plan and the efforts were geared at driving a collaborative approach to problem-solving that included managers, staff, parents, students, and community members. Assigning project management to emerging leaders is a great way to distribute leadership, manage change and develop leadership.

In Santa Ana, Haglund led the shift from minimal technology to high-access learning environments, and a top-down system of managed instruction districts to a portfolio approach where teams of teachers have the ability and responsibility to create coherent personalized learning models. Haglund supported the development of a new lab school formed as dependent charter in an incubator space near the central office. The project-based,

STEM-focused school is blended and competency-based with grades 4–6, and will continue adding grades to include grades 4–12. The school will move to a new location as it expands and the incubator space will go on to house other schools.

LEADING FOR DEEPER LEARNING: TIPS FROM DAVID HAGLUND

- **Lead with projects:** Distribute leadership across the organization and use projects to manage change and develop talent.
- **Support teacher teams:** Allow teacher teams to develop or select instructional models and support their decision with investment, technical assistance, and support.
- **Balance:** Empowerment agendas that balance improvement and innovation.

The leadership lessons from these five leaders are critical for a changing world where leaders have a new set of realities, roles and responsibilities. Here is a summary of eight implications for education leaders to consider:

The world is changing—fast. Work is dynamic and often gig (short assignment) or project-based. People live, learn, work, and shop on platforms. Automation is reshaping the employment landscape. Building and leveraging smart machines are new value-add opportunities. Education will need to stay nimble in terms of desired outcomes as well as practices, structures, and communication.

Lifelong learning is key—for everyone. "A learning organization is a place where people are continually discovering how they create their reality—and how they can change it," said

Jim May, Chief Schools Officer for the New Tech Network.

Leaders should hold community conversations about how the world is changing, and how to prepare in response to these changes. They should create partnerships with libraries, colleges, and employers that promote lifelong learning.

Leadership is no longer a title. Leadership should be distributed across the organization to create optimal learning environments for *all* stakeholders (students, teachers, families, and the organizational structures of schools). Leaders can help set the stage and improve or transform their organizations by managing change as a system of projects. Deeper learning requires community partnerships for community and work-based learning.

Leaders promote collective action. Leaders lead conversations that result in a shared vision of a better future. They work with all community members towards common goals. Those who model working together with the community will also be modeling the social and emotional skills required to interact in society.

Leaders make hard stuff possible. Leaders balance improvement and innovation by creating community agreements for progress. They break change into doable chunks of work backed up by support and resources. They encourage network participation inside and outside the district. They test big ideas in small, safe places.

Diverse work experiences build breath. They recognize the many and varied leadership roles and create their own path. You cannot rely solely on formal preparation or what's provided by an organization. Take responsibility for your own path. Draw a bigger sphere of influence. Apply for or create learning experiences, and seek out coherent leadership preparation.

Projects are integral to a leadership and talent development strategy. Leaders construct developmental experiences

SAFE AND PRODUCTIVE TEAMS

Project team effectiveness equals productivity. In 2012, Google launched a project code-named Aristotle to study why some teams worked better than others. After observing over a hundred groups for more than a year, they arrived at something unexpected—group norms. In particular, one factor stood out more than others: creating "psychologically safe environments." Teams that encourage safe discussions and different viewpoints succeed more. On the good teams, members spoke in roughly the same proportion, what researchers referred to as "equality in distribution of conversational turn-taking." The good teams had high social sensitivity; they had team members who could sense how others felt based on their tone of voice, their expressions, and other nonverbal cues. The Google finding suggests that it's not only important to learn project management, but that learning how to form teams and practice collaboration is key.

for themselves and others who carry out the organization's agenda and grow talent. Make real-time learning resources available to them.

Project-based development. Leadership preparation and professional learning should be aligned to and modeled after the types of project- based and deeper learning environments we seek to create for students.

School leaders are chief sense makers, interpreting district and network directives and offerings and, for as long as possible, creating clarity for staff members about priority outcomes and what supports are available.

Network leaders make decisions about where to be firm, and where to be flexible, and tend to focus on fidelity and innovation. Networks invest in tools that support core capabilities and continually attempt to improve their value proposition for schools. In dynamic networks, teachers feel supported, valued, and heard. Those who want to lead have opportunities to contribute.

NOTES

1. http://www.gettingsmart.com/publication/moving-pd-from-seat-time-to-demonstrated-competency-using-micro-credentials
2. http://www.gettingsmart.com/2016/11/give-teachers-experiences-want-students
3. https://www.amazon.com/College-Career-Ready-Helping-Students/dp/111815567X
4. https://www.youtube.com/watch?v=gzit15gCnMY&t=228s
5. http://www.gettingsmart.com/2016/01/personalizing-math-and-success-skills-in-brooklyn
6. https://www.usatoday.com/story/sponsor-story/xq/2017/03/20/one-brooklyn-school-wants-change-how-kids—-and-teachers—-taught/99403566
7. http://www.gettingsmart.com/2016/12/use-projects-manage-change-develop-leaders

IMPACT ENGINES

Picking the Right Business Model

Networks of aligned people have always been powerful, but now that they're all connected they operate a lot more like a live organism than a hierarchy. What comes with this new life form is a great opportunity to supercharge the social sector—how we support lifelong learning and provide youth and family supports.

Authors of Platform Revolution suggest that platform-based organizations beat the alternative because they scale efficiently by eliminating gatekeepers, unlock new sources of value

WHAT IS A BUSINESS MODEL?

A business model describes how an organization creates and delivers value (i.e., we serve X by doing Y). In the commercial sense, a business model describes products and services sold to a target customer group. In the social sector, business models often compliment philanthropic support to scale and sustain impact.

Are there business model innovations in the social sector?

Interest in reaching underserved audiences has lead to several innovative business models that leverage new technology tools:

- **Market development:** Intermediate organizations aggregate demand (for crafts, agriculture, AIDS drugs) to create new markets.
- **Entrepreneur support:** Training programs, incubators, and microlenders support startups.
- **Cost breakthrough:** Low-cost schools and services reach new markets.

through co-creation, use data to create community feedback loops, and invite users into the organization. Platforms that get better with each new user exhibit positive network effects. Large, well-managed platform communities produce significant value for each user by promoting valuable exchanges of information, goods, services, and currency. The ability to monetize the value exchange is crucial to a scalable and sustainable platform. Rather than developing content, many platforms rely on user co-creation and match content and connections at scale using algorithmic filters. Getting these core interactions right is the key to scale (think Facebook vs. MySpace). As co-authors, users are invited into platform operations.

Sangeet Choudary, co-author of Platform Revolution, offers 16 principles for digital transformation in his platform manifesto. Not all of them apply to impact organizations, but they signal a new way to achieve scale and organize enterprises.

PLATFORM MANIFESTO: 16 PRINCIPLES FOR DIGITAL TRANSFORMATION[1]

1. **The ecosystem is the new warehouse:** Scale is achieved through the efficient organization of ecosystems and processes towards value creation.
2. **The ecosystem is also the new supply chain:** Organize ecosystem resources and labor through a centralized platform coordinating actions.
3. **The network effect is the new driver for scale:** Scale is achieved by leveraging interactions in the ecosystem
4. **Data is the new dollar:** More data absorbed leads to more monetization opportunities.
5. **Community management is the new HR management:** Manage communities like distributed employees; enable the learning and development of producers.
6. **Liquidity management is the new inventory control:** Matching supply and demand efficiently is the only way that a platform can hold the two sides together.
7. **Curation and reputation are the new quality control:** From hierarchies for quality control to curation and reputation management.
8. **Users journeys are the new sales funnels:** A data platform unifies multiple touch points, enabling positive nudges along the customer journey.
9. **Distribution is the new destination:** Meet consumers by distributing services across their journey, planning for multi-point connectivity.

(continued)

10. **Behavior design is the new loyalty program:** Creating habits ensures users stick around. Network effects also create stickiness.
11. **Data science is the new business process optimization:** Shift from repeatable internal process to repeatable ecosystem interactions.
12. **Social feedback is the new sales commission:** Design social feedback to encourage producers on a platform.
13. **Algorithms are the new decision makers:** Algorithms leverage employees and ecosystem inputs to perform gatekeeping and resource allocation roles.
14. **Real-time customization is the new market research:** Serve the most relevant content from producers to interested consumers, and balance relevance with serendipity.
15. **Plug and play is the new business development:** application program interfaces (API) make it easy for applications to talk to each other, and are the contract and the integration interface.
16. **The invisible hand is the new iron fist:** Rather than hierarchal control, productive behavior is promoted through opt-in options and gradual nudges (through the invisible hand of data, algorithms and APIs).

Platforms create new way to think about scale, particularly impact at scale. While some of these new axioms may not seem to apply to leading a school or impact organization, consider these questions:

- Instead of focusing exclusively on internal issues and telling people what to do, could we focus more on edge/external interactions (e.g., parent involvement, student agency, donor engagement, partnership development, or community-based learning opportunities)? (#1, #2)

- How could we collect more and better data about our customer, client, and/or student interactions? (#5, #11–15)

- Instead of focusing all of our energy on employee evaluations, how might we leverage community feedback? (#5, #7)

- How might we encourage co-creation? When could consumers (clients, teachers, learners) become producers? (#5, #8)

- How might we study and improve the experience of our client or student? (#8, #10)

- Rather than imposing a change agenda on a hierarchy, how might we invite innovation and nudge progress? (#16)

NETWORKS NEED A BUSINESS MODEL

Impact initiatives start with a vision for a better state and plan for change. Increasingly, impact organizations are adopting network strategies, leveraging the power of platforms, and incorporating business models that support scale and sustainability. There are seven relevant business models for impact organizations:

1. **Philanthropic:** Direct services or advocacy supported by grants. Examples:
    i. *Advocacy:* Achieve, Alliance for Excellent Education, 50CAN, Edutopia
    ii. *School networks:* XQ, ConnectEd, YouthBuild
    iii. *Content:* Khan Academy, CK–12, Gooru, TED
2. **Public service:** Provide a public service with public reimbursement (shown in the right side of Figure 10.1).

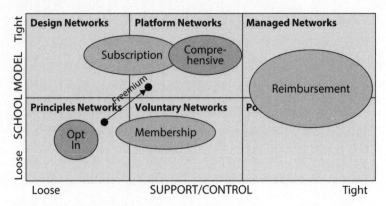

Figure 10.1 Typical business models

Examples: school districts and charter management organizations.

3. **Sponsored:** Advertisements or sponsorships to access the network. Examples: NPR, EverFi, and EdSurge.

4. **Subscription:** Users pay an annual fee to become a member or subscribe to access the network. The objective is long-term retention and recurring revenue. Examples:
   i. *Networks:* Big Picture, NAF, CAPS Network, EdLeader21
   ii. *Platforms:* i-Ready (adaptive learning), Canvas (learning platform)
   iii. *Content:* Education Week, Planet3, PLTW, AVID

5. **Comprehensive:** Subscription to a comprehensive school model including brand, platform, content, design services, and learning opportunities. Examples: Acton Academy, AltSchool, Cisco Networking Academy, and New Tech Network.

6. **Fee-based:** Earned revenue through direct sale of products or services. Examples:
   i. *Testing:* ACT, ETS, College Board, Measurement Inc.
   ii. *Marketplace:* Udemy, Teachers Pay Teachers (K–12), Top Hat (college textbooks)

7. **Freemium:** Users gain limited access to free resources (which may be supported by advertising) and pay a premium for added features; works well for online services with low acquisition costs but high lifetime value. Examples:

   i. *Platforms:* Edmodo, ClassDojo, Schoology, Moodle
   ii. *Content:* Open Up Resources, EL Education (professional learning services in support of open education resources)

The first four categories may use a platform. The last three categories leverage platform characteristics. While platforms are potentially powerful, not all of them achieve scale. Some nonprofits have tried membership platforms and freemium strategies unsuccessfully. Only a handful of impact organizations will achieve the viral growth and network benefits of massive platform networks, but every organization can benefit from thoughtful use of platforms including enhanced interactions, co-creation, and empowered frontline actors. There is no reason to impose a top-down hierarchy when a dynamic learning organization is called for and tools and examples abound.

CHOOSING THE RIGHT BUSINESS MODEL

Most networks are organized as nonprofit corporations and rely on fee-based income for operating support and philanthropy for research and development. Networks add value by getting bigger and better. Bigger networks create more interaction opportunities (e.g., a chamber of commerce adds more business members, and Coursera adds more university partners). Better networks create more value per transaction (e.g., Canvas adds video capabilities, and New Tech Network adds elementary grades). The critical success factor for any network is keeping perceived value greater than perceived cost.

Voluntary and managed networks experienced their most rapid growth when grants are available to support new and transformed schools (#1). While some older voluntary school networks have stalled, those that adopted platforms, transitioned to a membership structure, and cultivated dynamic edge interactions have thrived.

Platform networks usually operate like a franchise (#5)— they bundle a learning model, platform, and set of learning opportunities in a subscription agreement. Like software-as-a-service (SaaS) agreements, bundled services often improve over time through continually updated tools.

GREEN SCHOOLS: A CASE STUDY

If you wanted to create a network of environmentally friendly schools, you might create the Green Schools Alliance, an international membership organization of almost 8,000 schools. To join, one person signs up. The good news is that it's fast and cheap to build a big network. The bad news is that most schools won't change much just by signing a pledge or joining an association.

Jennifer Seydel has bigger ambitions. She wants to inspire a new generation of schools in low footprint healthy facilities, and she wants learning experiences that encourage young people to know, respect, and care for the world around them. In short, she'd like to change everything about school—and that is a much heavier lift than a pledge site. With like-minded colleagues, Jennifer began hosting an annual conference. The Green Schools National Network was formed to identify and support a group of schools that featured green buildings and healthy environments, and promoted environmental literacy.

Seydel has wrangled a dozen schools and a half a dozen districts committed to piloting, documenting, and sharing best practices. This broader agenda includes architecture, operations, and education. If she is able to raise some philanthropic capital to add technical assistance and implementation tools, the design network would become a platform network (as shown in Figure 10.2).

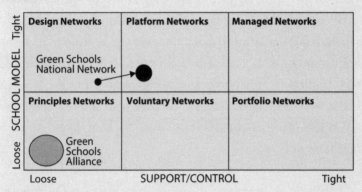

Figure 10.2 Green Schools case study

To support a more robust developmental and support agenda, the Green Schools National Network will likely need to adopt a membership model (or subscription model if it involves a technology platform).

These two networks have very similar themes, but different aims leading to different network strategies. The likelihood of schools to buy memberships and for foundations to offer sponsorship will also influence network decisions. Public policy, funding, or requirements may also impact network decisions. Picking the right business model and network strategy depends on many context variables.

As discussed in Chapter Eight, a growing number of curriculum providers like PLTW operate as platform networks with a point of view on the learning model, content shared on a platform, and several professional learning and collaboration options.

Toronto-based Top Hat offers an attractive alternative to expensive higher education textbooks with a marketplace of digital resources and authoring tools. Professors assemble online courseware by creating, borrowing, or buying content. Students pay a subscription fee to gain access to courseware that is usually much cheaper than traditional textbooks. This distributed co-creation model cuts out the middleman, allows content creators to earn a much larger share of the proceeds than traditional textbook authoring, and provides students with interactive, aligned, and affordable instructional materials.

While some networks sound like markets, keep in mind what networks require:

- **Affiliation:** Members or subscribers make an affirmative decision to associate.

- **Access:** Members or subscribers gain access to network resources (brand, services, information sources, premium content).

- **Interdependence:** The co-creation, transactions, and flows between members create mutual value.

Many impact organizations used mixed business models including philanthropic support (#1) to get started and design new programs and earned revenue (#6) or subscription (#5) to build a sustainable impact organization.

REMEMBER, SERVICE MATTERS

For schools thinking about platform-based services (whether whole school models or curriculum programs), remember that service is key. Service from the provider can make or break the experience of teachers and the learning outcomes of students. Service starts with the sales process but continues through implementation, ongoing support, and the life of the service partnership. School and district leaders should discuss service at length during the sales process, including account management, levels of service, data migration, rostering, and the product roadmap or plan for future enhancements.

Proactive service is as important as reactive service. For example, if there is a new district initiative, a good account manager will reach out to that district and serve as a partner in determining how the product can be a part of the solution. Providers should be "looking out for" their customers, and if a new feature has been added to their program, they should know how it applies and what it implies for every one of their customers. A good service provider also monitors a district's data to look for "stories" in the data that may be helpful in providing specific insights into the school or district's student performance.

Reactive service is about speed, accuracy, and personalization. Can a district easily call their account manager and ask them a quick question before the next class starts, or does the customer need to submit a "ticket" online or to someone who is not familiar with their special situation and wait 72 hours for an automated response? The service relationships should be as personal as the learning provided to the students. A strong partnership is key and communication between the district and the provider will make

(*continued*)

good service even better. It is important to cultivate ongoing relationships. A service purchased today, no matter how good it is, will be obsolete soon because of ever-changing curriculum requirements and technological advancements. It is important to focus as much on who you want to go on this journey with—and how well they can adapt—as you do on the current features.[2]

Some organizations start with one business model to prove core viability of their premise and then migrate to a second business model for scaling (e.g., AltSchool starting as tuition-based managed network and migrating to a franchise network).

Platform-powered networks hold the potential to create dynamic engines for good—better teaching conditions, better learning opportunities, better tools, and better supports—all propelled by leaner, smarter organizations.

NOTES

1. https://www.slideshare.net/sanguit/the-platform-manifesto-16-principles-for-digital-transformation/176-THE_PLATFORMMANI FESTOThank_You
2. http://digitallearningnow.com/site/uploads/2014/01/ Procurement-Guide-FINAL.pdf

GOVERNANCE

Use Networks to Boost Quality Options

Today, there are about 13,500 school districts in the US, serving over 47 million students. Ten percent of students are clustered in a dozen mega districts. The top 100 districts serve at least 40,000 students. These big districts face growing competition from charter, private, and homeschools, which now serve about 10 million students.

Next-generation learning incorporates blended, personalized, and competency-based learning with sophisticated designs and platform tools. Students in these new learning models, spend at least part of the day on their own learning journey engaging with tailored experiences, making it complicated to build and operate these environments without the benefit of a common platform.

As an alternative to a district-wide technology deployment, these networks are combinations of learning models, platforms, and professional learning adopted by individual schools or feeder patterns. For example, eight middle and high schools in El Paso, Texas are part of the New Tech Network.

With a combination of local, state, and federal funds, school districts spend an average of $11,000 per pupil, ranging from a low of about $6,600 in Utah and Idaho to over $20,000 in New York.[1] As taxing entities, school districts can also borrow money for capital construction and repay it with a levy on local property tax.

There are three general operating models for school districts—enterprise, shared decision-making, and portfolio models. They roughly correspond to size—most of the 12,000 small districts are enterprise models, most medium districts are some version of shared models, and most large districts are portfolio models.

Enterprise: Borrowing a business term, an enterprise approach implies common goals, processes and tools. Enterprise districts (like managed school networks) share goals and a learning model (curriculum, assessment, and teaching practices); a common school model (structure, schedule, and staffing); information systems, learning platforms, and access devices; and professional learning opportunities.

Enterprise districts define the *what* students should know and be able to do and *how* they will learn and demonstrate learning. Coherence and efficiency are the primary benefits of an enterprise approach. In systems of managed instruction, this may feel highly directive and come with pacing guides and benchmark assessments. A single approach may not work for all learners and the system may lack agility and ability to innovate.

Some enterprise districts like the Mooresville Graded School District distribute leadership, and give teachers a voice inside the organization and a role in sharing success externally. In a dynamic enterprise system, change is top-down, bottom-up, inside-out and outside-in.

Shared decisions: Most districts operate in the middle ground where the central office makes some decisions, schools make others, and some are negotiated. An example follows:

In many districts, decision-making appears to be ad hoc, relationship-based, and or poorly documented (i.e., it's never quite as succinctly laid out as the chart would have you believe), leading to resentment and a lack of role and goal clarity.

District-Defined *What*	Shared/Negotiated Decisions	School-Defined *How*
• Standards & graduation requirements • Opening/ closing schools • Accountability/ intervention • Schedules & transportation • Facilities management • Employment contracts	• Core curriculum • Assessments • Student progress • Professional development • Learning platform • Access devices	• Instructional strategies • Electives • Supplemen- tal materials • School climate • Extracurriculars • Student sup- port strategies

Medium and large districts have schools in several performance categories. To rationalize supervision and services they often create performance categories and provide tiered support.

Good schools can opt out of services and struggling schools get more directed support (districts like Cincinnati under Steven Adamowski and Boston under Thomas Payzant were early adopters of this tiered support model). In a well-executed tiered support system, school performance defines its relationship with the district and potential for earned autonomy may add to unique educational options for families.

As in Houston, this tiered support system may be augmented by themed and magnet schools to expand student and family options—but this can also create resentment towards schools that receive special treatment.

A shared decision-making model with categories of tiered support is complicated to construct and operate, especially during periods of change (which is most of the time).

Portfolio: A city with multiple school operators is (to borrow a term from finance) a portfolio—whether accommodative or antagonistic. Most big districts are portfolio districts but they vary in the extent to which they embrace or resist charter schools.

An urban portfolio includes purpose-built schools as well as historical neighborhood schools. Purpose-built schools and networks are important, according to Don Shalvey, because it's easier than taking apart and rebuilding existing schools. It also moves the goalposts, redefining what is possible beyond the current state, so that the outrageous becomes fair game.

A district that acts more like an authorizer than an operator, and where most budget and operating decisions are made at the school or network level is using a portfolio strategy. Robin Lake, Center for Reinventing Public Education, said, "The portfolio strategy tries to harness the best ideas for creating

DON SHALVEY ON DISTRICT-CHARTER RELATIONS

In his fifth month as San Carlos Unified superintendent, Shalvey took advantage of a new charter school law to open a lab school. Shalvey notes that every big company has an R&D department, but districts don't usually have a place to innovate. The second charter school in the country provided the district an opportunity to "play in future perfect tense" and experiment with multi-age grouping, new staffing strategies, and technology-enabled learning.

In 1998, California modified the charter school law to allow one board to manage a multi-campus network. With Netflix CEO Reed Hastings, Shalvey launched Aspire Public Schools, one of the first charter management organizations designed to scale. Today, Aspire is one of the largest and most successful school networks in the country, serving 16,000 mostly low-income students in 40 K–12 schools in California and Tennessee.

According to Shalvey, purpose-built schools and networks are important, because it's easier than taking apart and rebuilding existing schools. It also moves the goalposts—the moment you create something that appears to be outrageous, "anything in between what currently exists and that outrageous thing becomes fair game."

After retiring as the CEO of Aspire, Shalvey joined the Bill & Melinda Gates Foundation as their ambassador of district-charter collaboration. He launched the Compact Cities initiative, a network of 22 communities where school districts peacefully coexist and work together on common problems including foster youth, overage and under-credited students, young parents, and learners with special needs.

(continued)

Notable partnerships including Spring Branch ISD in metro Houston and their partnership with KIPP and YES to better serve African American youth. Hartford Public Schools works with Achievement First on a leadership preparation. The compact in Denver focuses on teacher-to-teacher collaboration. Unique factors spur these partnerships—sometimes crisis, sometimes opportunity, always thoughtful leadership. Mayors can be catalytic. The late Tom Menino was critical to sustained progress in Boston. Michael Hancock was instrumental to collaboration in Denver.

What's the future of school networks? Shalvey is excited about empowerment zones and networks of district innovation schools. He points to Shelby County iZone in Memphis Tennessee, the multiple operator approach to turnaround in Lawrence Public Schools Massachusetts, and to Beacon Schools, a network of innovation schools in Denver.

ownership at the school level, and in parent choice, community engagement, and government oversight with one end in mind: quality public education for every student."

Denver Public School's portfolio approach keeps district innovation and charter schools on a level playing field when it comes to incubation, funding, enrollment, transportation, and accountability. In Santa Ana, California and Fulton County, Georgia, teams of teachers have the ability and responsibility to create coherent personalized learning models and devices that support their plan.

A portfolio strategy, advocated by the three dozen nonprofit regional members of Education Cities, leverages the capability of school networks and multiple operators to create options for families. Where there is collaboration, a common enrollment, discipline, funding, and facilities plan can be used.

WHAT CAN SCHOOL DISTRICTS LEARN FROM CHARTER MANAGEMENT ORGANIZATIONS?

Alex Hernandez, from the Charter School Growth Fund, says school districts can learn three lessons from great charter school networks:

1. Define what excellence looks like—a shared vision for powerful learning experiences—and build an organization completely in service of that vision, from hiring to training to coaching to curricula development.

2. Districts should make the investments necessary so schools across the system can become world-class in chosen areas. Sometimes that means building new infrastructure in-house, but for most districts this means using infrastructure built by other high-performing school systems or support organizations. This process works best when the central team provides training and resources that schools find useful and, in turn, classroom educators improve those resources for the rest of their colleagues based on what is working for the kids.

3. Large school districts could shift their focus from operating schools to authorizing high-quality networks of schools. At some point school districts can get so large, that getting adults to agree on a concrete vision for classroom excellence becomes nearly impossible. Districts can empower networks of schools to can align around a vision for excellence and resource them to build the infrastructure they need to make their schools great.

Portfolio managers may proactively seek options for underserved geographies and groups.

A portfolio can be confusing to middle managers if the school district is both operator and authorizer. As one district innovation officer said, department heads "continue to attempt to exert their positional authority rather than act as service providers."

Denver Public Schools offers an incubator, the Imaginarium, to teacher teams from district and charter schools.[2] Districts like Denver attempting to incubate new learning models and scale successful charter and innovation networks find the philanthropic requirements challenging.

Cities with a portfolio of options can be overwhelming to parents if they, like New York City, include hundreds of options. The more options that exist, the more important it is to have a parent and student information and enrollment system in place.

District leaders should be clear and articulate about their strategy. Every school leader should have clarity on the organizing ideas for their school—whether unique or common across a district or network. They should have a clear picture of how things should work, and who makes what decision, so that they can create clarity for teacher roles and goals.

Unique factors spur these partnerships—sometimes crisis, sometimes opportunity—but always, thoughtful leadership is in play. Mayors can be catalytic. The late Tom Menino was critical to sustained progress in Boston, Massachusetts. Michael Hancock was instrumental to collaboration in Denver, Colorado.

Almost every big urban city has a portfolio of educational options. Many of the big city school districts don't acknowledge much less collaborate with the competition. Yet as educational choice, technology, and "anywhere anytime" learning become more inevitable, a collaborative portfolio strategy that takes advantage of school networks (both inside and outside the school district) is the only option that makes sense.

NOTES

1. http://www.governing.com/topics/education/gov-education-funding-states.html
2. http://www.gettingsmart.com/2017/03/getting-smart-podcast-denver-public-school-system-exemplifies-a-healthy-educational-ecosystem

POWERFUL
LEARNING AT SCALE

Inspiration and Intermediation

"We believe that investing in and catalyzing the personalized learning field can lead to bigger breakthroughs in education."
—New Profit partner Trevor Brown

Seasoned teachers know that teaching requires making hard choices about what is most worthy of time and attention. This is particularly true of project based learning where time is created for exploration of a driving question. These daily academic questions not only reflect a sense of priority but a theory of education. Exposing students to the organized out-line of adult understanding does not magically deposit that knowledge into a student brain for future use. The failure of the coverage model suggests focus on a set of priority out-comes. This question of "depth vs. breadth" does not need to be made class by class, but it is one of the benefits of networks where careful and shared deliberation has yielded a set of priority outcomes.

Teachers across the New Tech Network focus on five priority outcome areas: Knowledge and Thinking, Written Commu-nication, Oral Communication, Collaboration, and Agency. They share Learning Outcome rubrics for assessing student work products. These rubrics unpack each skill dimension in detail. For example, Agency includes "using effort and prac-tice to grow" and "seeking challenge." Collaboration includes subskills like "team and leadership roles." These rubrics were created in collaboration with groups like the Stanford Center for Assessment, Learning, and Equity, and represent research on the key skills needed to be successful in academics and beyond.

Networks have a shared conception of what it means to be educated, of what to learn, how to learn, and what forms of demonstration are valued. These decisions about what it means to be prepared and how young adults develop most frequently surface when contemplating new schools.

DEVELOPING NEW SCHOOLS

New school development was the most important improve-ment strategy of the last 20 years leading to higher achievement and graduation rates. The focus was replicating quality learn-ing environments for underserved students and communities.

Ten years ago there were not a lot of new tools, and new schools were most commonly the old fashioned version of school with a focus on rigor, relevance, and relationship (the Big Picture mantra). In addition to thousands of charter schools, school districts opened thousands of new schools, particularly high schools. It was typically effective at producing high test scores and graduation rates, but slow and expensive.

When venture investment started flowing into education in 2010, many of the startups followed the social media formula—offer a free product, iterate to promote viral adoption, and eventually find ways to monetize the network effects. This West Coast formula has been only partially successful as a business model, but it did create a new backdoor to the classroom for teachers, students, and parents who found and deployed free and open resources. The flood of new tools helped to create a wave of blended learning, some remarkably innovative learning models—and a lot of confusion.

Education technology startups cluster around investors and technology talent in the Bay Area, New York, and Chicago. Conversely, innovations in learning sprang up anywhere there was visionary leadership (e.g. Mooresville, North Carolina, Columbus, Mississippi, and Chugach, Alaska). Yet it can be difficult to scale these innovations without an entrepreneurial context.

Inspiration: Time for a road trip

New purpose-built schools not only create quality options, they inspire others to explore what's possible. Visiting new (and transformed) schools may be the best form of professional development.

Seth Andrew founded Democracy Prep, a network of 17 high-performing schools in New York, New Jersey, the District of Columbia, and Baton Rouge, educating over 5,000 citizen-scholars.

Reflecting on his leadership preparation, Seth found his $60,000 Harvard degree the least valuable investment. "It failed on every level," said Andrew. It was philosophy and theory and nothing specific about running great schools. More practical was his Building Excellent Schools fellowship. "Experience was most important," said Andrew. He visited 30 different schools including KIPP, Northstar, and Frederick Douglas Academy to see what "good" looks like.[1]

Similarly, Joseph Erpelding, principal at the innovative Design39 in southern California shared that making about 30 school visits with two other administrators was his most valuable preparation experience. Now Erpelding is inspired by visiting high-tech San Diego area businesses.

Aaron North, Vice President of Education at the Ewing Marion Kauffman Foundation, said, "The national interests may want to take a look at the collaborative efforts emerging in Kansas City. . . . In the last eighteen months, more than 300 people from a broad cross-section of the community have been part of visits to cities with concentrations of high-performing public schools."[2] The Kauffman funded initiative, KC Great Schools, brought diverse groups of teachers, district and charter administrators, and business and civic leaders to visit high-performing and innovative schools in eight cities. The goal of these trips is to create a sense of what is possible and to inspire Kansas City leaders to collaborate on new school development and transformation.

As a philanthropic strategy it is both wise and brave. Compared to directly funding proven providers—a sure bet that will benefit few—Kauffman is promoting city-wide learning and collaboration, a strategy likely to pay big dividends, but in ways hard to predict.

MATT BERTASSO ON INSPIRATIONAL SCHOOL VISITS

Matt Bertasso's journey began with school visits, where he began to imagine what is possible. After visiting Rochester High School in northern Indiana, Matt was sold not by the computers, but by the engaging project based learning. He saw students diving into their learning in ways he had rarely seen before. He saw the agency and engagement again at other Indiana schools in the New Tech Network, and knew it was worth investigating.

After adopting the New Tech model in Oregon-Davis Schools and implementing in the 9th and 10th grades, the change to the entire school was invigorating, and he started to see the real potential of what project based learning could achieve. "The culture changed. The work changed. We changed," said Matt.

Having done his undergraduate work in Idaho, Matt jumped at the chance to open a New Tech school in Idaho Falls. "One of the best parts of the NTN model," said Matt, "is that it allows for innovation within the model." Compass Academy operates like a software development company constantly iterating on the design to improve student progress. The school has a culture of change with a staff that values adaptability.

Intermediation: You need a friend

Old schools don't change easily. New schools aren't developed quickly. New learning models are promising, but increase the degree of difficulty. What will transform this sector?

There is an important layer for schools—a set of services that provides inspiration, design, incubation, funding, and rapid feedback. This important conclusion of the Smart Cities study is that an innovation intermediation layer will prove crucial for next-generation learning at scale. It is new, intermediary organizations that are creating productive ecosystems where innovations are more likely, better supported, and have a chance to scale.

School networks like New Tech Network and other local innovation intermediaries can play the first four roles. The last six roles create a healthy regional ecosystem. As an added benefit, beyond building individual education startup and innovation communities, these catalysts are central to bringing diverse stakeholders to the table and kickstarting locally driven solutions.

The work of these innovation intermediaries is to advance the pace of innovation and break down silos in education. This layer will pave the way for greater communication and standard operating procedures for launching new education solutions. And it will aid in sharing and scaling ideas and talent across the community, with catalysts adapting these things to their local context.

It will take local knowledge, trust, and community-building to surface, support, and scale innovations in each market. Those same ingredients are crucial as well to forging a strong foundation and connecting early adopters. Beyond that, an active community that builds the capacity to innovate will enable more and more educators, parents, students, and communities to join the ranks of early adopters, and possibly become innovators themselves.

10 INTERMEDIARY FUNCTIONS

- **Design:** Support for developing a learning model and school model (Highlander Institute, Getting Smart, and Transcend).
- **Technical support:** Selecting a learning platform, developing technology stack aligned with a learning model, expanding broadband access, and building a support model.
- **Professional development:** Teachers need learning opportunities linked to the design and technology choices (Buck Institute, Bloomboard, Edivate).
- **Talent development:** Recruiting and leadership developing great talent is critical to improvement (TFA, TNTP, Education Pioneers, Leading Educators).
- **Grants:** Local support and guidance for new learning models (NGLC Regional Funds, Silicon Schools, NewSchools Catapult, and XQ Super Schools).
- **Incubation:** Capital, space, technical assistance and organizational development for startups (4.0 Schools, LearnLaunch, ImagineK12).
- **Catalyst:** Organizations that are embedded and trusted locally and connected nationally that serve as a convener and bridge (The Lean Lab, Highlander Institute).
- **Harbormaster:** Ecosystem coordination, advocacy, and convening (Education Cities).
- **Seed:** Early stage support for education technology startups (Reach Capital, Kapor Capital) and venture funding for growth companies (Rethink Education, Owl Ventures, Reach Capital, Kapor Capital, GSVlabs, Learn Capital).
- **Feedback:** Access to schools for short cycle trials and pilots (LEAP Innovations, Digital Promise).

There are a growing number of healthy local ecosystems of innovators across the country and a mesh of connections and national networks:

- *Strive Together* is using collective impact strategies to align local stakeholders in three dozen cities to a common vision of better education.

- *Digital Promise,* with initial support from the US Department of Education, launched Education Innovation Clusters, a loose network of two dozen metro areas promoting innovations in learning.

- *Mozilla Hive* is powering local Learning Networks and Communities around web literacy (e.g., Hive Learning Network in NYC, which provides an array of intriguing learning experiences for middle and high school students).

- *Village Capital* launched a program to enable ecosystem leaders to build better resources to support entrepreneurs.

- *LRNG* is a national nonprofit connecting youth with out of school work and learning opportunities.

These layers of inspiration, incubation, and intermediation between schools and entrepreneurs is what will ultimately expand access to innovative learning environments, and create aggregated demand for investment and new tools—and fuel the learning revolution to come.

NOTES

1. http://www.gettingsmart.com/2017/01/podcast-special-ed-teacher-to-white-house-tech-advisor
2. http://www.kansascity.com/opinion/readers-opinion/guest-commentary/article134522379.html

ADVOCACY

A Nation Proud of Its Public Schools

Advocacy aims to change hearts and minds. Advocacy seeks to shape decisions impacting political, social, and economic systems. Advocacy has a view of what's working and why. Advocacy imagines that the future can better for more people.

Lobbying—a case made to power—is the most direct form of advocacy. It may be called "education" if it doesn't include a specific request for money or language, but it's still an effort to change heart and minds. Making the case for change requires a compelling vision. It helps to have a track record of success. And, it almost always needs to be a sustained drum beat over what might be years of telling the story.

There are three specific forms of advocacy that achieve scaled impact. The first is jointly funded projects. Foundations can lobby the federal government for new programs if they help foot the bill. These jointly funded projects can provide a big return on effort. In 1998, Mott Foundation entered into a public-private partnership with the U.S. Department of Education to support the country's 21st Century Community Learning Center program. This partnership led to increased funding for the program from $40 million to $1 billion as part of No Child Left Behind (NCLB).

The second is public-private partnerships. State investment can help bring early innovations to scale. Inspired by Kaiser Foundation investments, Oklahoma has a universal preschool program (despite terribly low funding for K–12). The Texas High School project (now Educate Texas), a partnership between the state and two national foundations, resulted in more than 130 high-quality STEM and early college high schools. The goal of the state and privately sponsored Computer Science for Rhode Island (CS4RI) is to have Computer Science taught in every public school by December 2017. The RAMTEC robotics training program launched in Marion Ohio expanded to 23 sites as a result of an Ohio Straight A Fund grant.

The third approach, pioneered by the Great Schools Partnership, is a triangular approach to advancing proficiency-based (or competency-based) learning. The Great Schools Partnership undertook this by building the New England Secondary School Consortium, and working with six New England legislatures on proficiency-based graduation requirements, gaining support for proficiency-based diplomas from 70 public and private

POLICY INNOVATORS NETWORK TO GROW IMPACT

Policy Innovators in Education (also known as the PIE Network) launched in 2006, connecting leaders of 15 advocacy organizations from 12 states. Since then, the PIE Network has grown to more than 80 organizations advancing education reform in 35 state capitals as well as Washington, DC, along with 20 national partner organizations.

The PIE Network, connected by Executive Director Suzanne Tacheny Kubach, is primarily supported by foundations who prioritize policy change. "We're a maximizer. When new initiatives, such as ESSA, break, they know the PIE Network's established communication patterns are essential," said Kubach. "And just as importantly, insights flow back to those investors."

Kubach has found that true networks are driven by different incentives than hierarchical organizations. While hierarchies can inhibit the flow of information that fuels innovation, the flat, collaborative structure of the PIE Network means "ideas and insights move rapidly in all directions, improving as they spread," said Kubach.

That key difference is why networks are so essential in building movements. "The reality of movements is that no one is in charge," Kubach noted. "My team does not have 'line authority' over any Network member, yet we convene working meetings, and collect and spread insights and resources. Often that sparks sustained, collective action."

Kubach underscores a point made in Chapter Two. "The most powerful glue of a network is trust: that's earned every day and something we can never take for granted. It also requires relentlessly proving the value for participation and giving back."

education institutions in the process. By working with all stake-holders simultaneously, Great Schools Partnerships removed typical excuses (e.g., colleges won't accept, states won't allow).

More subtle is work done well and shared broadly. Civic engagement is advocacy. Social service is advocacy. Active citizenship is advocacy. A school that breaks barriers and extends equity is advocacy—a proof point that provides evidence of a claim. Public work products and community connections are important forms of advocacy for a school.

Advocacy usually focuses on *what* and *why* (e.g., all students deserve to be college and career ready) in the early adopter phase, and shifts to *why* and *how* through the point of majority support (e.g., curriculum programs and guidance strategies).

Joining a network is also advocacy. Networks form community—a commitment to learn and improve together. When communities of practice produce favorable working conditions and remarkable life outcomes across hundreds of schools in widely varying conditions, that's more than a proof point—it's a movement.

HOW DO GOOD IDEAS SPREAD?

Theories of how change happens in the social sector consider the demand for change, the attributes of innovation, the complexity of change, and how it impacts people.

Demand for innovation. How people discover and come to desire the product or practice and the role of communication and decision-making, particularly among those rouge innovators. The traditional distribution curve suggests that innovation is spread from innovators to early adopters, to early majority and late majority, and finally, those pesky laggards.[1] This process is supposed to be a function from knowledge, persuasion, decision, implementation, to confirmation.

Diffusion is something that happens to a gas in a vacuum or a fad in a culture, but it is not a very good explanation of how innovation happens in education. The traditional curve proposed by Everett Rogers in 1962 is more appropriate for individual actors adopting new products or practices.[2] Individual teachers usually have some autonomy to adopt new practices and free products. But education has layers of context variables that make real progress lumpier and more episodic. While robust ecosystems create supportive conditions for innovation, school and system leaders that facilitate agreements among communities of practice remains an important part of the process. Where leadership exists, innovation can flourish. Where it does not, it is squelched.

Attributes that promote innovation. There are seven main factors that influence adoption of an innovation[3]:

- **Relative Advantage:** The degree to which an innovation is seen as better than the idea, program, or product it replaces.

- **Compatibility:** How consistent the innovation is with the values, experiences, and needs of the potential adopters.

- **Complexity:** How difficult the innovation is to understand and/or use.

- **Triability:** The extent to which the innovation can be tested or experimented with before a commitment to adopt is made.

- **Observability:** The extent to which the innovation provides tangible results.

- **Adaptable:** The extent to which the innovation can be adapted to a particular context.

- **Scalable:** The balance between elements scaled easily and those requiring infrastructure (e.g., human resources, finance, technology, and governance).

Personalized learning, especially aimed at deeper learning competencies, has high advantages but also high complexity, low triability, adaptability, and scalability. And given the limited ability to measure broader aims (i.e., mindsets, creativity, and collaboration), personalized learning has limited observability.

The big advantage of school networks is that they bundle innovations, reducing complexity and boosting adaptability and scalability. They range from lightweight design networks like Future Ready Schools that just require a pledge to a set of principles, all the way to managed networks which ensure classroom-by-classroom fidelity to a learning model.

As personalized learning platforms get more robust, they will make it easier for schools to support sophisticated learning sequences. For example, Cortex, developed by New York nonprofit InnovateEDU and piloted at Brooklyn LAB, is an extensible platform that supports a variety of personalized learning models.

Change management. Innovation diffusion is a function of the complexity of the system and the ability of incumbents to manage the adoption process. Rogers argues that innovation that is complex, ambiguous, or unfamiliar will be slow to spread—and unfortunately that characterizes personalized learning. Despite the complexity and confusion, personalized learning has become the dominant meme in US education. Interest is high but models are early, and implementation is often weak.

School districts and networks can boost change management capacity by breaking their transformation process into a series of projects and distributing them across the organization to aspiring leaders who would benefit from a challenging assignment and breadth of exposure challenge. David Haglund, superintendent in Pleasanton, California, said that "It is a very cool way to spread the message about managing a 21st-century workflow in the organization, and resets the thinking of the adults to be aligned to the instructional shifts tied to project based learning implementations."[4]

Behavior modification. Innovation that requires behavior change is a much heavier lift than an innovation that reinforces existing behavior. Roger's model, proposed in 1962, is most applicable to consumer adoption of new products (more than stopping behaviors). Rogers (and more recently others) have suggested behavior change is a function of information, motivation, and conditions.

Public health studies suggests that innovation diffusion varies depending on the nature and complexity of the innovation, costs and incentives, communication channels, and the social context.[5] Like health, youth development is influenced by a complicated mixture of influences including peers, family, school, and community.

New outcome frameworks like MyWays from NGLC describe the knowledge, skills, and dispositions most important to civic and career success. MyWays stresses self-direction, social skills, positive mindsets, surveying the landscape, and navigating each step. But a relatively small percentage of youth have access to experiences that promote these basic skills outcomes. The know-how exists to create good schools that promote these next-generation outcomes, but less is known about transforming struggling schools. Organizations like New Tech Network that partner with public districts are helping to address the school turnaround challenge.

HOW INNOVATION SPREADS IN EDUCATION

- **Innovation in teams:** Practices and products (especially when free) spread quickly to individual teachers, but quality learning opportunities for a community require shared practices and tools adopted by school teams and systems. Fads are easy; real innovation takes gravity-defying leadership.
- **Uneven progress:** Development of innovative bundles of practices and tools (like personalized learning) is complicated at this stage, so progress is lumpy, leader-dependent and context specific—not a smooth diffusion curve.
- **Why innovate?** Clarity on desired outcomes, specific experiences that develop those outcomes, and agreement on feedback/measurement will speed adoption.
- **Better tools:** Platforms that simplify design and adoption of new learning models will speed adoption.
- **Networks help:** Like-minded schools sharing innovation bundles (clarified outcomes, tools, and professional learning) may not speed adoption, but improves fidelity. Networks can amplify your voice and leverage your work.

SYSTEM HEADS AS ADVOCATES

Many school superintendents come to see themselves as chief advocates for their districts—making the case internally and externally with stakeholders for a change agenda. Some campaigns are formal elections that require subtle support (given legal prohibitions); others are district-led campaigns to build teacher or partner support. Education leaders build and spend political capital to support their advocacy agenda.

The Winton Woods City School District is located just a few miles north of Cincinnati and serves a diverse student population of more than 3,800 students. Of them, 14% are English Language Learners speaking 26 different languages, more than 85% identify as ethnic/racial minorities, and 74% of students qualify for free or reduced lunch. With the support of an Ohio Straight A Fund Grant, Winton Woods began implementation of the New Tech model across the entire district, with all schools Pre-K to 12 using the NTN model of project based learning by the 2018–2019 school year.

"After an extensive evaluation of project based learning in conjunction with the New Tech Network, it was a natural progression to offer this experience to all of our students. Educators have a daunting task of leading reform efforts while working with students to promote equity. This is exactly what the New Tech Network experience will do for our students," said Superintendent Anthony Smith. "We have a golden opportunity to teach our students how to become problem solvers while exceeding state standards. We are excited about our educational framework that will help to develop well-rounded learners."

Retired Cross County School District (featured in Chapter Five) superintendent Carolyn Wilson recognized that her rural students needed access to the same career education as urban youth. With support from the New Tech Network, her team created a college and career course, virtual internships, and counseling support to and through college.

In El Paso, Texas, Superintendent Juan Cabrera turned a district from a myopic focus on test preparation to a city that embraces active learning aiming at an updated graduate profile. Cabrera created a partnership with the New Tech Network to augment his team's capacity and create new options (discussed in Chapter Six).

In Denver, Colorado, Superintendent Tom Boasberg led the development of a new graduate profile and a plan to help all students achieve this high level of success (discussed in Chapter Eleven). Networks are an important part of the Denver plan—both innovation networks and charter networks. All of Denver schools operate on a level playing field with comparable policies for enrollment, discipline, and funding.

These four superintendents are strong advocates for children. They support and leverage school networks to improve the quality and variety of options available to families.

Network advocates

Leaders of school networks advocate for their students, their schools, and their approach—which often includes limits to required testing and the opportunity to extend impact.

Limited testing: School networks typically share elaborate assessment systems and have constructed tools for combining multiple formative assessments to inform learning, to make judgments, and to guide system improvement. These networks know how every student is doing in every subject, every day—they don't need to take a week off in the spring to test them to find out what they know and can do. Most school networks would gladly demonstrate the efficacy of their assessment system and, like the New York Performance Standards Consortium, would appreciate a waiver from state testing systems.

Weighted funding: Access to public funding that is relevant to the level of challenge is key to success in serving challenging populations. Schools that serve a large percentage of students that bring multiple risks to school should receive more funding than schools that serve well-supported youth.

Expanded impact: Networks seek the ability to expand where need and demand exists. That could include district partnerships and/or supportive and rapid authorization. It always includes the need for public and private philanthropy to support new school development or school transformation.

Public school pride

We see a future a where young people aren't just preparing for a distant future, but taking up serious challenges and producing positive impacts in their communities today; where the work students do makes them, their families, and their communities proud. We see a future where parents in all communities feel confidence and excitement for the learning journeys their students face.

Personalized learning is promising but challenging. If this work was a straightforward technical challenge, you could follow a cookbook. But this work is adaptive with shifting targets and evolving opportunities. Working in networks provides low-risk entry points, support for strong implementation, and the opportunity to contribute.

The aim of the New Tech Network is to become a nation proud of its public schools. With hundreds of New Tech affiliated schools and thousands of like-minded networks and school districts, we see this aim not just as possible, but critical. This is the equity and economic development issue agenda of our time.

NOTES

1. Rogers, Everett G. (2003). *Diffusion of Innovations, Fifth Edition.* New York, NY: Free Press.
2. Everett G. Rogers, (1962). *Diffusion of Innovations, First Edition.* New York, NY: Free Press.
3. Adapted from Billions Institute: www.billionsinstitute.com
4. http://www.gettingsmart.com/2017/04/projects-that-learn
5. http://sphweb.bumc.bu.edu/otlt/MPH-Modules/SB/Behavioral ChangeTheories/BehavioralChangeTheories_print.html

APPENDIX

Networks, Schools, and Tools Mentioned

School districts and networks mentioned

- Achievement First, www.achievementfirst.org
- Acton Academy, http://actonacademy.org
- Alpha Public Schools, www.alphapublicschools.org
- AVID, www.avid.org
- AltSchool, www.altschool.com
- Aspire Public Schools, http://aspirepublicschools.org
- AppleTree Institute, www.appletreeinstitute.org

- Big Picture Learning, www.bigpicture.org
- Brooklyn LAB Charter Schools, www.brooklynlaboratory school.org
- Beacon Network, https://beaconnetworkschools.org
- Blue Valley School District, https://district.bluevalleyk12.org
- CAPS, www.bvcaps.org
- CAPS Network https://yourcapsnetwork.org
- Carmen Schools of Science and Technology, www.carmen highschool.org
- Chicago International Charter School, www.chicagointl.org
- Coalition of Essential Schools, http://essentialschools.org
- ConnectEd, www.connectedcalifornia.org
- CottageClass, http://cottageclass.com
- Da Vinci Schools, www.davincischools.org
- Democracy Prep Public Schools, http://democracyprep.org
- Denver Public Schools, www.dpsk12.org
- DSST Public Schools, http://getcollegecredit.com
- EL Education, http://eleducation.org
- EdLeader21, www.edleader21.com
- Evergreen Elementary School District, http://evergreen .ccsct.com
- Harmony Public Schools, www.harmonytx.org
- IDEA Public Schools, www.ideapublicschools.org
- International Studies Schools Network, http://asiasociety.org/ international-studies-schools-network
- Internationals Network for Public Schools, http://interna tionalsnps.org

- Kettle Moraine School District, www.kmsd.edu
- KIPP, www.kipp.org/
- Rocky Mountain Prep, http://rockymountainprep.org
- Fresno Unified School District, www.fresnounified.org
- FutureReady, http://futureready.org
- Harmony Public Schools, www.harmonytx.org
- Hartford Public Schools, www.hartfordschools.org
- High Tech High, www.hightechhigh.org
- IDEA Public Schools, www.ideapublicschools.org
- Lawrence Public Schools, www.lawrence.k12.ma.us
- Leadership Public Schools, www.leadps.org
- League of Innovative Schools, http://digitalpromise.org/initiative/league-of-innovative-schools
- LRNG, www.lrng.org
- Mastery Collaborative, www.masterycollaborative.org/#home
- Match Education, www.matcheducation.org
- School District of the Menomonie Area, http://msd.k12.wi.us
- National Academy Foundation (NAF), http://naf.org
- New Tech Network, https://newtechnetwork.org
- New Visions for Public Schools, www.newvisions.org
- Next Generation Learning Challenges, http://nextgenlearning.org
- Oregon-Davis School Corporation, http://odschools.org
- Project Lead The Way (PLTW), www.pltw.org
- Salisbury Township School District, www.salisburysd.org
- Santa Ana USD, www.sausd.us

- Shelby County iZone, www.scsk12.org/izone
- SPARK Schools, www.sparkschools.co.za
- STRIVE Preparatory Schools, www.striveprep.org
- Summit Public Schools, www.summitps.org
- Summit Learning, www.summitlearning.org
- Success Academy, www.successacademies.org, and its Education Institute http://successacademies.org/edinstitute
- Remake Learning Network, http://remakelearning.org
- RAMTEC, www.ramtecohio.com
- Rocketship Education, www.rsed.org
- Mooresville Graded School District, www.mgsd.k12.nc.us
- TeachersPayTeachers, www.teacherspayteachers.com
- Teton Science Schools, www.tetonscience.org
- Thrive Public Schools, www.thriveps.org
- Poway USD, www.powayusd.com
- Porterville USD, www.portervilleschools.org
- Los Angeles USD, www.lausd.net
- Udemy, www.udemy.com
- Urban Assembly, http://urbanassembly.org
- Van Wert City Schools, www.vwcs.net
- West Des Moines Community Schools, www.wdmcs.org/district/our-schools
- Wildflower Schools, wildflowerschools.org
- Winton Woods City School District, www.wintonwoods.org
- Wonderschool, www.wonderschool.com
- XQ Institute, https://xqsuperschool.org

- YES Prep Public Schools, www.yesprep.org
- YouthBuild, https://youthbuild.org

Individual schools mentioned

- Academy of Science & Entrepreneurship, www.mccsc .edu/ase
- Belleville New Tech High School, MI, http://bellevillenew tech.com
- Boston Day and Evening Academy, www.bacademy.org
- Compass Academy, https://compassd91.wordpress.com
- Cross County High School, AR, www.crosscountyschools .com
- Cesar Chavez Multicultural Academic Center, www.chavez .cps.edu
- The Community School, http://www.spokaneschools.org/ Domain/1251
- Decatur Central, http://www.msddecatur.k12.in.us/central-high/new-tech
- Design39Campus, http://design39campus.com
- Design Tech High School, CO www.designtechhighschool .org
- Denver School of Innovation and Sustainable Development, http://dsisd.dpsk12.org
- e3 Civic High, www.e3civichigh.com
- EPIC Elementary, http://epic.liberty.k12.mo.us
- GCE Lab School, IL, https://gcelabschool.com
- Cougar New Tech at Franklin High School, TX, http:// franklin.episd.org/new_tech

- Greenville Early College, SC, www.greenville.k12.sc.us/ec
- Global Freshman Academy, www.edx.org/gfa
- Horace Mann Elementary, www.horacemanndc.org
- Katherine Smith Elementary, CA, https://krs.schoolloop.com
- Mesita Elementary, TX, http://mesita.episd.org
- New Technology High School, https://www.newtechhigh.org/
- Nex+Gen, NM, http://nexgen.aps.edu
- NuVu in Cambridge, MA, https://cambridge.nuvustudio.com
- One Stone, ID, http://onestone.org
- Palo Alto High School, CA, www.paly.net
- Phoenix Coding Academy, http://www.phoenixunion.org/coding
- Roots Elementary, http://rootselementary.org
- Rochester High School, http://rhs.zebras.net
- Quest Early College High School, www.humbleisd.net/qhs
- Sacramento New Tech, www.sacnewtech.org
- Science Leadership Academy, www.scienceleadership.org
- Singapore American School, www.sas.edu.sg
- Olin College, MA, www.olin.edu
- Samueli Academy, CA, http://samueliacademy.org
- Quest Early College High School, www.humbleisd.net/qhs
- Vista High School, http://vhs.vistausd.org
- Washington Discovery, IN, www.plymouth.k12.in.us/washington
- Workshop School, www.workshopschool.org

School support and advocacy groups mentioned

- 4.0 Schools, http://4pt0.org
- 50CAN, https://50can.org
- ACT, www.act.org
- Achieve, www.achieve.org
- Alliance for Excellent Education, http://all4ed.org
- Bill & Melinda Gates Foundation, http://gatesfoundation.org
- The Colorado Education Initiative, www.coloradoedinitiative.org
- James Irvine Foundation, www.irvine.org
- Broad Foundation, http://broadfoundation.org
- Building Excellent Schools, http://buildingexcellentschools.org
- Buck Institute for Education, https://www.bie.org/
- Bloomboard, https://bloomboard.com
- Edivate, http://www.schoolimprovement.com/products/edivate
- Chan Zuckerberg Initiative, www.chanzuckerberg.com
- Charter School Growth Fund, http://chartergrowthfund.org
- College Board, www.collegeboard.org
- Center for Reinventing Public Education, www.crpe.org
- Digital Promise, http://digitalpromise.org/
- Edutopia, www.edutopia.org
- Educause, http://educause.org
- Education Cities, http://education-cities.org/
- Education Pioneers, www.educationpioneers.org

- Education Week, www.edweek.org
- ETS, www.ets.org
- ImagineK12, www.imaginek12.com/
- William & Flora Hewlett Foundation, www.hewlett.org
- Highlander Institute, www.highlanderinstitute.org
- Carnegie Corporation, www.carnegie.org
- Carnegie Foundation for the Advancement of Teaching, www.carnegiefoundation.org
- CityBridge Foundation, www.citybridgefoundation.org
- Great Schools Partnership, http://greatschoolspartnership.org
- Getting Smart, http://gettingsmart.com
- GSVlabs, http://gsvlabs.com
- IDEO, www.ideo.com
- iNACOL, www.inacol.org
- Kapor Capital, www.kaporcapital.com
- LearnLaunch, http://learnlaunch.com
- LEAP Innovations, www.leapinnovations.org
- National Writing Project, https://www.nwp.org
- New England Secondary School Consortium, http://new englandssc.org
- Next Generation Learning Challenges (NGLC), http:// nextgenLC.org
- Michael & Susan Dell Foundation, www.msdf.org
- LEAP Innovations (Chicago, Illinois); www.leapinnovations .org
- New Schools for New Orleans, www.newschoolsforneworleans .org

- Owl Ventures, www.owlvc.com
- Policy Innovators in Education, http://pie-network.org
- Rogers Family Foundation, http://rogersfoundation.org
- Reach Capital, http://reachcap.com
- Rethink Education, http://rteducation.com
- Stanford d.School, https://dschool.stanford.edu
- SRI, www.sri.com
- Transcend Education, www.transcendeducation.org
- Teach for America, www.teachforamerica.org
- XQ Institute, https://xqsuperschool.org
- TNTP, https://tntp.org
- Leading Educators, www.leadingeducators.org
- Silicon Schools, www.siliconschools.com
- NewSchools Venture Fund, www.newschools.org
- The Lean Lab, http://theleanlab.org

Tools mentioned

- Blackboard, www.blackboard.com
- Cortex, InnovateEdu, www.innovateedunyc.org
- Canvas, Instructure, www.instructure.com
- I-Ready, Curriculum Associates, www.curriculumassociates.com
- MasteryConnect, www.masteryconnect.com
- Ed-Fi, www.ed-fi.org
- Edmodo, snapshot.edmodo.com
- Engrade, www.engradepro.com

- Empower Learning, empowerlearning.net
- EverFi, http://everfi.com
- JumpRope, www.jumpro.pe
- Teacher2Teacher, https://teacher2teacher.education
- Teachers Pay Teachers, www.teacherspayteachers.com
- Khan Academy, https://www.khanacademy.org
- CK–12, www.ck12.org
- Gooru, www.gooru.org
- Summit Learning, www.summitlearning.org/
- TED Conferences, LLC, www.ted.com
- Minecraft: Education Edition, https://education.minecraft.net
- Mozilla, www.mozilla.org
- Motivis Learning, https://motivislearning.com
- Planet3, http://exploreplanet3.com
- Open Up Resources, http://openupresources.org
- OpenEd, ACT, www.opened.com
- TopHat, https://tophat.com
- PowerSchool, www.powerschool.com

INDEX